EXPERIENCES OF PLACE

Center for the Study of World Religions
Harvard Divinity School

Religions of the World
General Editor: Lawrence E. Sullivan

Cambridge, Massachusetts

EXPERIENCES OF PLACE

EDITED BY
MARY N. MACDONALD

Distributed by Harvard University Press for the
Center for the Study of World Religions
Harvard Divinity School

Book design by Eric Edstam

Cataloging-in-Publication Data available from the Library of Congress

ISBN 0-945454-37-6 (hardcover)
ISBN 0-945454-38-4 (paperback)

CONTENTS

ACKNOWLEDGMENTS

From mulling over ideas for a lecture series back in the spring of 1999 to publication of a book containing the lectures, it has been a pleasure to work with the staff of the Center for the Study of World Religions at Harvard Divinity School. I would like to thank Dr. Lawrence Sullivan, director of CSWR, who readily accepted my suggestion of a lecture series focused on experiences of place and the history of religions. Before the lecture series began, and as it unfolded, Malgorzata Radziszewska-Hedderick, then coordinator for educative planning at the center, and her assistant, Brooke Palmer, made all the arrangements that enabled the lectures to take place. I am very grateful to them for the care with which they contacted speakers, arranged for flyers and publicity, and welcomed those from Harvard and the wider community who attended the lectures. As we listened to the lectures, the idea of turning them into an edited volume emerged and was enthusiastically supported by Kathryn Dodgson, senior editor at CSWR. Kit worked with us with sensitivity to our ideas and with patience for our foibles as we turned a series of lectures into an edited volume. All the contributors are thankful to her and to Eric Edstam who designed the book and the cover featuring Uluru (Ayers Rock), a site sacred to Aboriginal Australians. Each of the authors has particular debts of gratitude to family members, friends, and colleagues who encouraged and supported them in their writing. To all who helped to bring these reflections on experiences of place to publication we give our warm and heartfelt thanks.

INTRODUCTION:
PLACE AND THE STUDY OF RELIGIONS

MARY N. MACDONALD

In the 1999–2000 academic year it fell to my happy lot as a visiting professor at the Center for the Study of World Religions at Harvard University to organize a lecture and colloquia series entitled "Experiences of Place and the History of Religions." In suggesting the theme, I had in mind that place and orientation are important aspects of human experience and significant components in conceptions of religion. Moreover, several important articles and books giving attention to place had recently appeared and it seemed a timely topic.[1] Over the course of the year seven lecturers – Ann Grodzins Gold, Steven Feld, Nili Wazana, Jacob Olúpònà, Mary Gerhart, Michael Barkun, and Deborah Bird Rose – invited us to reflect on the significance of places, real and imagined, in the traditions they study. Six of those lectures are brought together in this collection. Each suggests that place is of fundamental importance in the ways that people orient themselves to the world and negotiate their passages through life.[2]

Place – the word evokes geography and culture; it conjures up history and myth. Feeling at one with a particular terrain, we say we have a sense of place; body and mind come to grips with their environment. A sense of place includes a sense of community. We might experience a solidarity with others who occupy a particular city or prairie or forest "place" and look to them for the networks of support which enable us to make our way in life, or we might experience the people and animals and vegetation of our region as competitors in our effort to forge a place for ourselves. For some people one place is dominant in their lives; for others a number of places are significant. Of course, our responses to places change over time. We construct and deconstruct and reconstruct places. A desert that appears austere and lifeless to a newcomer may, to the attentive inhabitant, be nourishing and aesthetically appealing, a place teeming with life and possibility. While "place" evokes the reality of our material situation, it also raises for a large number of people the hope for a not yet realized security. Although human beings may yearn for a place to call their own, or for a place superior to their present location, many people in fact find themselves out of place in situations of exile or diaspora. Some are torn between two or more places.

Place is not only a particular physical location, but also an idea, a mental construction which captures and directs the human relationship to the world. Place is significant for the study of religion because religious traditions work with concrete and imagined places in constructing worlds of meaning. We find ourselves "in place" and we also try to create a place for ourselves. There is an immense variety of ways in which we come to place ourselves. We place ourselves geographically, psychologically, socially, chronologically, spiritually. Some ways of placing ourselves are more fruitful and functional than others; some are quite dysfunctional. The papers in this volume discuss how places are known, imagined, remembered, and struggled for, and their significance for orienting human lives. The papers share the perspective that places are conceived of and constructed by human beings. Each investigates the ways in which a particular place has been understood by those who inhabit it, visit it, or contemplate it.

THE CONCEPT OF PLACE

On the surface the notion of place seems straightforward. We might say a place is a locality or a physical environment, a space which human beings have converted into a meaningful habitation. Place, however, means more to us than a physical location. Place is not just a spatial, or even a spatial *and* temporal, notion; it is also a poetic and aesthetic conception and a political strategy. We bring places to play in building meaningful worlds and communities and invest them with cultural and religious meanings. Places are human constructions that come into being when people act on space. As Allan Pred has suggested, place is "a historically contingent process" which appropriates and transforms space and nature.[3] Place enables us to bring a number of our life's concerns into focus; place generates personal and cultural identity. Place may also be the focus of political, ethnic, and religious struggle.

Cultural geographers have given attention to the way that human communities work with place. Anne Buttimer, for example, proposes that we should think about places in terms of home and horizons of reach:

> I suggest we think about places in the context of two reciprocal movements which can be observed among most living forms: like breathing in and out, most life forms need a home and horizons of reach outward from that home. The lived reciprocity of rest and movement, territory and range, security and adventure, housekeeping and husbandry, community building and social organization – these experiences may be universal among the inhabitants of Planet Earth.[4]

Buttimer's formulation of home and horizons of outward reach is not unlike the perspective of the Solomon Islands anthropologist David Gegeo. In an article published in 2001, at a time when ethnic strife in the Solomon Islands had forced Malaita Islanders living and working on Guadalcanal Island to return home, he describes what "place" means to someone from Kwara'ae on the island of Malaita.

> First and foremost, place (*kula ni fuli*, literally, "place situated in source," that is, place of one's existential foundation) in this context refers to the geographical or physical location of Kwara'ae district on Malaita. Second, place refers to genealogy, that is, one's location in a Kwara'ae kin group, both in the present and reaching backward and forward in time. Third, place means having land or the unconditional right of access to land in Kwara'ae through genealogy and

marriage. Fourth, place means the unquestioned position, based on genealogy and marriage, from which one may speak to important issues in Kwara'ae without being challenged about identity or the right to engage in dialogue, such as during a communal meeting.

Fifth, place means native fluency in both registers of Kwara'ae language, that is, *ala'anga kwalabasa* 'low rhetoric' (informal register; literally, "meandering, unimportant speech") and *ala'anga lalifu* 'high rhetoric' (formal register; literally, "importantly rooted speech"; Watson-Gegeo and Gegeo 1990, 1991). Sixth, place means the assumption that because one is already defined as Kwara'ae, one is knowledgeable about Kwara'ae culture, history, cosmology, ontology, epistemology, and so on. Seventh, place is accompanied by certain kin obligations and responsibilities that cannot go unfulfilled, and from which one is freed only by death. Such responsibilities include contributing to brideprice or bridewealth payments in marriages, uniting with one's kin group in times of land or other major disputes and for communal projects, and contributing food and other necessities to the family of a kin member who dies.

Eighth, place means that one shares Kwara'ae perspective(s) through which to view and transform social reality, and be transformed by it – that is, one shares Kwara'ae indigenous ontology and epistemology. Ninth, place means knowing cultural models and having a Kwara'ae cultural framework such that even if one is born and raised in another space, on going to Malaita one can quickly make sense of and acquire depth in aspects of Kwara'ae cultural knowledge that one previously did not know. The framework makes rapid learning possible.[5]

Gegeo reflects on migration patterns in the Pacific and on the possibilities of being rooted in place, yet free to move to other places and to return to the home place. In the long term the island of Malaita has insufficient resources to support all who claim it as home, so he predicts that some will be obliged to seek employment elsewhere for at least part of their lives. For him this does not erase their indigenous identity or their ties to place. He argues that "identity and place are portable."[6] Similar claims are made by other peoples who are obliged, because of economic circumstances or war, to dwell outside their homeland but yet identify themselves in terms of home place. Some people who leave behind their home place do not have the possibility of return or choose not to return. In many cases, though, the new place of the immigrant is constructed in terms of the old place, or at least in a way which remembers the old place even as a new place comes into being. All over the world we find place names derived from migrants' former towns and regions, some of them with the prefix "New" – New York, New London, New Orleans, New South Wales, and so on. New places are also named after imaginary or literary places, persons who populate such places, and events portrayed in them.

Experiences of colonialism and forced relocation have often shifted notions of place. For many Native Americans the reservation, not the original homeland but a negotiated space reflecting a history of oppression, has become the locus of community life. Both Buttimer and Gegeo in their different ways make the point that the human experience of place involves movement between the home place or primary place and places of extension or reach. For the immigrant physical return may not be possible, but nostalgia for a remembered place – the Old Country – now reconstructed in the light of subsequent experience may continue to shape the life of an individual or community.[7] The attachment to a home place seems to be significant for many people, but there are other ways to think of how we inhabit places. In highly mobile societies, such as that of the United States where 20 percent of the population moves every year, movement from place to place may mean that the place of birth and childhood is left behind and that people focus on present location. In recent years an emphasis on human responsibility for the ecological crisis has led many people to focus both on the health of the particular habitat in which they are located and on the situation of the planet. Thus, environmental activists are encouraging development of an ethics of place which applies wherever human beings find themselves.

SELF AND SOCIETY IN PLACE

There is no doubt that the construct of place is important for the establishment of both personal and communal identity. The philosopher Gaston Bachelard maintained that the relationship between person and place is so intimate that someone seeking to understand himself or herself might be helped more by topoanalysis, that is, by an exploration of self-identity through an analysis of the places in which one has dwelt, than by standard psychoanalysis. Bachelard reflects on the localization of memories, particularly in terms of the house or houses in which one has lived.[8] Following his lead one would revisit the rooms of a house in which one has lived to recapture what happened in them and the emotional tones of the experience. Although not many of us enter explicitly and systematically into such a process of analysis of places, the sensory events of our daily lives trigger memories of the places in which we have dwelt and thus help us to remember whence we have come and how we have been shaped. For instance I, who spent my earliest years on a dairy farm in rural Australia, am transported in memory to that place by encountering farm animals at the New York State Fair, by seeing and tasting cumquots and mangos from a supermarket, by observing eucalyptus trees in South Africa, or by smelling the frangipani scent of a candle. Other sense experiences – the smell of skunk, the taste of blueberries, the sight of fields of corn – will recall Central New York, my current place of residence, even if I happen to be elsewhere. Synesthetically, I am linked to the places of my life. Were I to follow Bachelard's suggestion, I might walk in memory around the farm where I lived as a child, revisit the lecture halls and seminar rooms and the Great Court of the University of Queensland, and recall the places in Papua New Guinea where I have shared food and stories with friends.

Cultures the world over have mapped the geographical world according to the topography of the human body. In the English language we speak of heads, necks, shoulders, and mouths as features of the human body and also as aspects of landscape. Similarly, in Melanesian languages in which I have worked, one word serves for grass and hair, one for knee and mountain, for nose and hill, for river and artery, for eye and lake. In describing the ways the people of the Lelet Plateau of the New Ireland Province of Papua New Guinea organize space and place, Richard Eves observes:

> Images of the body pervade Lelet conceptualizations of the way the world is constructed and inhabited. The use of corporeal tropes is an important part of the process by which these people develop attachment to their place (*lemenemen*). They construct a cosmology of

space and place around the contrasting images of bodily comport-
ment, especially those of an immobile body and a mobile body.[9]

The homologous linking of person, society, and cosmos which is common
in the work of Melanesian healers points to cosmologies in which health
is construed as a good economy of exchange in the personal body, the social body, and the cosmic body and in which illness is construed as a bad
economy of exchange. Self and community are thus understood to participate in the configuration of the larger place or cosmos. However, the
configuration of person, society, and cosmos is never final. Things go
wrong with the embodied and emplaced self, with society, and with the
cosmos. Out of dissatisfaction with a clogged-up, painful, or enfeebled
system arises a desire for change. Religious rituals are among the
processes which facilitate change and "replacement."

As well as exploring personal attachments to place, one can also inves-
tigate social associations of place and political values of place. Place

Fig. 1. Mt. Giluwe: Kewa narratives tell of quarrels between Mountain Giluwe, Mountain Ialibu, and Mountain Sumale (Murray), the three mountains that dominate Kewa
territory in the Southern Highlands of Papua New Guinea. In one tale Giluwe has his
teeth smashed in by Sumale, resulting in his jagged appearance today. (Photo: Mary
MacDonald)

serves not only as a basis for the development of personal identity, but also as a nexus for the convergence of social, religious, and political traditions. It connects the individual to the processes of state and culture.

SACRED PLACE

Studies in religion make use of the categories of sacred place and sacred geography. Since Mircea Eliade (1907–1987), it has become common to speak of sacred time and sacred space or sacred place.[10] In Eliade's formulation a sacred place is understood as a place which is distinguished from ordinary or profane places. It represents a discontinuity with the places of ordinary life and is a location where the sacred will become manifest. Thus, his understanding of sacred space or sacred place depends on affirming the category of the sacred, which he defines as the "opposite of the profane."[11] Eliade uses the term "hierophany" for manifestations of the sacred. "When the sacred manifests itself in any hierophany," he writes, "there is not only a break in the homogeneity of space; there is also revelation of an absolute reality, opposed to the nonreality of the vast surrounding expanse. The manifestation of the sacred ontologically founds the world."[12] Sacred places are often venues set aside for ritual action. Eliade presents them as places where the ordinary and the powerful, the profane and the sacred meet. He also suggests that sacred and profane may be two different modes of occupying space. It could be argued that Eliade's opposition of the sacred to the profane perpetuates Western dualisms and is not sufficiently attentive to the social and economic circumstances in which a place comes to be regarded as a repository of power and spiritual value. Nevertheless, Eliade's designation provides a framework for considering the significance of particular places for religious communities.

Eliade begins *The Sacred and the Profane* with reference to the work of theologian Rudolf Otto (1869–1937). Otto reflected on the fact that some places exert a particular power on those who enter them and evoke emotional responses of awe, fear, and attraction. He believed that an experience of the numinous underlies all religion and may be revealed in particular times and places. Otto called that which is revealed *Das Heilige*, the Holy, and described it as the *mysterium tremendum et fascinans*,[13] the terror-provoking or awe-inspiring, yet attractive or gracious, mystery. For

Otto, travel beyond Europe to Asia and to Africa nurtured an interest in religions other than Christianity and particularly in Hinduism. His use of the Holy as a cross-cultural term pointed to the role of emotion – a sense of the uncanny, feelings of dependence, an attraction toward the numinous – in religion.[14] Moreover, his emphasis on religion as experience paved the way for studies that would go beyond the cognitive claims of religions and would permit us to study experiences of place as religious phenomena.

Some places are specifically constructed for the gathering of devotees and the facilitation of their interaction with the divine. Thus we have temples, churches, mosques, synagogues, shrines, Sun Dance lodges, and cultic houses of various kinds. These are places where something happens. Many constructed sacred places are places of assembly in which, for example, people may gather for common prayer or sacrifice. In *The Hermeneutics of Sacred Architecture* Lindsay Jones writes of "the advantages of constituting interpretations of sacred architecture, not in terms of the meanings of buildings per se, but in terms of what are designated 'ritual-architectural events,' that is, occasions in which specific communities and individuals apprehend specific buildings in specific and invariably diversified ways."[15] He argues for shifting the focus from built forms to "monumental occasions" in which the built forms participate. A Gothic cathedral may be built to reveal an ideal order, with balance and harmony reflecting divine beauty and with proportionality and light employed to imagine heaven, but it is also constructed as a place for ritual exchange between the divine and the human. In considering places that are not specifically constructed but which are understood to be "naturally" imbued with power or to have associations with mythic ancestors or culture heroes, we might follow Jones's lead and focus not so much on the particular formation – river, mountain, grove, field, cave – as on the ritual events enacted there. Indeed, by an exercise of the religious imagination and by the performance of ritual, any constructed or natural place can become a sacred place.

Thus far I have given attention to the value of location. In *Map Is Not Territory* Jonathan Z. Smith points out that while religious traditions may value place, they may also discount or attempt to overcome location. He contrasts what he calls locative and utopian visions of the world. The locative vision, he says, emphasizes place while the utopian vision attempts to transcend place.[16] Smith sees the locative as normative and the utopian as a peripheral, disruptive tendency.[17] Both tendencies may be found in the same religious traditions. For example, a Muslim may orient herself or himself toward Mecca and go on pilgrimage to the places associated with the foundation of the religion and at the same time believe that this earthly place is but temporary and that real value resides with Allah in heaven. "All the world is a mosque," goes one Islamic saying. In other words, any place can be a place to worship Allah. However, Allah is not contained in any place but is beyond the world. While a universalizing tradition such as Islam may be resistant to localization, even the so-called world religions are formed in reciprocity with their local environments and exist with a tension of local and universal dimensions.

Places evoke various responses depending on personal and cultural development and religious commitments. It is rare that we apprehend a place without prior cultural and religious conditioning. A place which became significant because of something that happened there is not necessarily physically appealing. And a place which once was beautiful might no longer be so, but yet maintain its grip on the religious imagination. Thus, the devotee is moved by the Ganges River at Banaras, dirty as it may now be, apprehending it as part of a larger tradition and perhaps as a highlight of a pilgrimage to Banaras which also includes visits to many beautiful shrines and the company of fellow pilgrims. For the study of religion it is important that particular places that people regard as sacred or holy be studied. It is also important to consider the ways the earth or the cosmos is viewed as sacred or is made sacred through ritual.

SACRED GEOGRAPHY

Implicit, and at times explicit, in the oral and written narratives of religious communities is what scholars have come to call sacred geography, a mapping of a landscape which gives prominence to sources of sacred power. The term "cosmography" is similarly employed for the mapping of the larger world. Valuable as the notion of sacred geography may be, it is important to recognize that sacred geography overlaps economic and political geography. The placing of sacred sites may, for example, have significance for food supply and for governance.

Certain places are powerful or sacred, as we have seen, because of ritual performed there. Myth may also make a place sacred. Each culture has its collection of narratives which explain cultural origins and the activities which established places for the use of human beings and for the interaction of human beings with the gods, spirits, and culture heroes who first shaped their world. The narratives may refer to the known, regularly traversed landscape. They may also include imagined places known only through the telling of tales. In narratives, time and place coalesce so that we might speak of time-place, or, as is more frequently done, of time-space. In order to describe the articulation of time and place in the novel, Mikhail Bakhtin coined the term "chronotope."[18] By chronotope he refers to the balance of temporal and spatial in a unit for analysis. In literature the image of the person is, he says, "always intrinsically chronotopic."[19] Many peoples consider that their land was shaped by mythic ancestors or beings of an earlier time. In Japanese tradition, for example, it is told that the divine couple, Izanagi and Izanami, looked down upon the waters, dipped a jeweled spear into the ocean, and from its tip let drop the brine from which the first island of Japan was formed. Some cultural narratives also relate the role of historical ancestors in constructing their place in the world.

Let us consider two examples of sacred geography, that of Aboriginal Australia, which is further elucidated in Deborah Bird Rose's chapter, and that of the Inca, in order to see how the religious conceptualization of place renders it powerful and meaningful. Among the Australian Aborigines prior to and beyond colonial contact, nomadic bands traveled within defined tribal areas to find seasonally available food. The landscape they traversed was said to have been shaped in the Dreaming, a time of origins in which culture heroes wandered the land. The Dreaming, as Rose tells us, still exerts a powerful presence. Sacred sites within a community's territory designate places where events of the Dreaming took place. The narratives linked to places tell of the shaping of a water hole or a hill, the emergence of plants, the making of animals, the giving of laws. Thus, a people's sacred history, land titles, and law could all be read and told from the landscape. In addition to natural features, sacred geographies include human creations, such as, in the case of Aboriginal Australians, pictographs etched in caves and on stones. The carrying out of rituals at certain locations where the heroes of the past paused on their journeys links a living community to the generations that have preceded it and to the powerful forces which shaped the land and continue to provide nourishment to those who dwell in it and care for it.

The Incas told of a series of creations and destructions of a three-tiered universe. Above the earth were the heavens and below was the underworld. The earth was an arrangement of shrine places (*huacas*) surrounded and supported by local kin-based groups. Central to Incan sacred geography was the concept of *huaca*. In the Quechua language *huaca* means a person, place, or thing which is out of the ordinary, whether for beauty or ugliness or humorous qualities. *Huacas*, such as mountain peaks, springs, cliffs, unusual stones and plants, delineated a sacred landscape. Cusco, the Inca capital, was the center of the universe. More than three hundred important *huacas* in the vicinity of Cusco were conceived of as lying along forty-two lines called *ceques*.[20] *Ceque* is the Quechua word for line or border. The Incas divided the earth into quarters, the dividing lines of which intersected in Cusco. Like the rays of the sun, *ceques* radiated outward from the Coricancha, the principal temple of Incan state religion in Cusco, further dividing the quarters into districts, and perhaps symbolizing the outreach of the sun god and the ruler. As well as organizing sacred places, the *ceques* were also important in regulating social relations and economic life. The sacred sites, the *huacas*, were assigned to the care of local groups. Like the earth, the heavens were also divided into quadrants and the Incan agricultural and ceremonial calendars were regulated by the movement of heavenly bodies through the quadrants. The *ceques* also served as sight lines for astronomical observations. With the emplacement of Catholicism in the Andes, the old sacred and political geography and its ritual system were replaced but not completely destroyed.

In both the Australian and the Inca cases, economy, social relations, and religion are interrelated within a known place. The material and the mythic support the life of a local community. Philip Arnold's study of the cult of Tlaloc, the pan-Mesoamerican deity of rain and fertility, makes a similar point. Arnold locates the cult not only in the imaginative life of the Aztec people but very much in their material life as well.[21] "The Tlaloc cult," he says, "demonstrates that substantive dimensions of human existence are embedded in an ongoing contact with the phenomenal world.

Indigenous practices are not sentimental or spiritual. In an indigenous context, meaningful orientation to a living landscape constantly acknowledges, by ritual means, contact between living beings."[22]

COMPARATIVE PERSPECTIVES ON PLACE

Each of the six papers gathered in this volume highlights certain aspects of the study of religion from the viewpoint of place. Together they underscore that place is constructed in the intersection of material conditions, political realities, narrative, and ritual performance. Not only does each tell an absorbing story of a particular place; they all indicate directions we might take in the study of religion and place.

In a study of narratives commenting upon a deserted place in Rajasthan, Ann Grodzins Gold says that she is "interested in the ways religious realities interact with political ones in mutually transformative fashion." In exploring a set of tales relating to the Owl Dune, and another set of place tales concerning two deities, she finds that historical research is necessary to understand the place and its import. She is dealing with real people in a real landscape and considers the telling of tales to be part of people's negotiation of the material and political circumstances of life. The tale of a guru's curse causing the wood of the *dhokarā* trees to be crooked may seem to be just another etiological legend, but an exploration into the background of the curse locates it in the relationships of the groups occupying the region. Tales told by the Minas (former "tribals") assert that in the past they were the dominant caste and that the outsider Rajputs came later and usurped their authority. Gold demonstrates that at both the village and the state level, ritual performances for gods and goddesses are integral to group identity. She found in her study "that landscapes, inhabitants, and oral tales existed in relationships of mutual construction." Thus, she suggests, place in North India is not fixed but is a matter of negotiation, with tales of the Owl Dune bearing witness to a history of resistance and flux. Moreover, the tales bear a moral import suggesting "that the foods of life must be shared for society and nature to prosper safely; and that the line between rulers and bandits is a very fine one."

Whereas Gold worked mainly with oral narratives, Nili Wazana leads us in an analysis of written biblical texts concerning the Promised Land

and emphasizes the need to understand the literary forms employed in talking about place. In exploring literal and literary images of the Promised Land, she demonstrates the tension that exists between clearly defined territorial units such as we would display on a modern map and literary descriptions of a land and emerging nation such as we find in the Bible. Since biblical ideas about place have constituted one strand in struggles for the modern state of Israel – Zionist visions of land, labor, and liberation constituting another powerful strand – Wazana's investigation of ancient Hebrew literary images is relevant in thinking about contemporary conflicts over the borders of modern Israel. However, more important is her contention that the "from . . . to" passages (e.g., from Dan to Beer-sheba and from the Wilderness to the Sea) in the Pentateuch should not be read as boundary descriptions but as spatial merisms, synecdoches in which a totality is expressed by two contrasting parts. Merisms, she explains, can express totality by extreme members, but also by characteristic members. "The spatial merisms in promise terminology," she concludes, "reflect a land that has no borders at all, only ever-expanding frontiers; they are referring to universal rule using stock terminology of Neo-Assyrian royal inscriptions."

Jacob Olúpònà is committed to finding appropriate methods for the study of African religions and, like Ann Gold, emphasizes the importance of materiality as an entry into religious constructions. His chapter, "A Sense of Place: The Meaning of Homeland in Sacred Yorùbá Cosmology," shows how both myth and ritual reinforce a Yorùbá community's bond to its land. He quotes a Yorùbá proverb, "While the owners of a place tread very gently on it, the stranger treads very roughly," to demonstrate the view that the sacredness of place evident to the insider is not obvious to the outsider. In African religions, he suggests, the sacred is localized and to study it one needs to study particular places. In a frequently told and cited Yorùbá origin myth, the creative power of the Supreme Being, Olódùmaré, is transferred into the environment and becomes available in particular at places where sixteen Yorùbá gods take up their abodes. Ilé-Ifè, the city where creation took place, is regarded as the mother of all cities, as "the place where the structure and meaning of the sacred cosmos was first unraveled," and it is a place of both origins and ending. It is both the source of life and the place through which the dead pass on their journey to their life as ancestors. Olúpònà describes the layout of the city, with the royal palace at the center, to show how it connects people to the three realms of the Yorùbá cosmos and also supports Yorùbá nationalism. Similarly, he shows how the divination tray is a replica of the cosmos and facilitates connection of earth and heaven. He also gives attention to the role of new places, such as the Nigerian capital Lagos, in the negotiation of contemporary Yorùbá identity.

To many people at the beginning of the twenty-first century, perhaps particularly to scholars of religion, heaven is a place in the realm of imagination, a metaphorical place. However, in discussing the twelfth-century Sibyl of the Rhine, Hildegard of Bingen, Mary Gerhart faces the fact that in Hildegard's time and place heaven was construed differently. She contends that "Essentially, 'Heaven' for Hildegard was an integral part of the universe." It was "an aspect of the experience of transcendence in and through particular events and places." In reconstructing Hildegard for a modern audience, Gerhart first takes us to places in which Hildegard lived her life. Gerhart herself visited some of the places in which Hildegard lived – grounding herself as it were in the locatedness of the nun's life – and she shares her own impressions of those places as well as her research into historical records concerning them. She focuses on "Hildegard's idea of Heaven as the most complex treatment of place in her work," pursuing the precritical idea of heaven which emerges in Hildegard's accounts of her visions, in her cosmology – which as one would expect in twelfth-century Europe, does not separate the scientific and the religious – and in the liturgical songs she composed. As in many religious traditions, music for Hildegard was a means of bridging earth and heaven and of producing an experience of heaven in the here and now.[23]

Michael Barkun also takes us to places that many of us would regard as fantasized rather than real. These are places existing in the minds of believers who see the world in conspiracist terms and which we might regard as more troubling and more difficult to understand than Hildegard's experiences of heaven. In an exploration of myths of the underworld in contemporary American millennialism, Barkun works largely with literature produced in subcultural groups which tells, for instance, of battles raging between good and evil. Some of the beliefs about underworld places are, he says, "built around fundamentalist religion, some around extreme right-wing politics, and some around occult and esoteric teachings." Many of the underworld places which Barkun's conspiracy theorists describe are locations of battles either going on now or yet to come, but they are sometimes also places of retreat for the forces of good. The ingredients of the belief systems which posit underground locations and alien evil inhabitants range, says Barkun, "from deviant science and theosophy, to fringe bible commentary and fantasy literature." To begin to understand the construction of such places requires insight into the social and political as well as the religious processes which significant numbers of people find alienating and untrustworthy.

Like Jacob Olúpònà, Deborah Bird Rose is concerned with experience and knowledge of a particular place. Australian Aboriginal culture, she tells us, is all about place and, therefore, she defines religion in terms of place: "The genius of place is at the heart of religion, defined as engagements with the origins and deep patterns and processes of the created world." Aborigines speak of their "country," that is of the territory in which there are sites at which their Dreaming beings stopped on their journeys and in which they periodically carry out rituals. The bond between person and country is such that the person is responsible for keeping the country alive, just as the country supports the person's and the community's life. While the concept of place has provided a useful point of entry into the various religious worlds considered in the lecture series, it seems that the study of Aboriginal religion would be impossible without it.

In the 1990s religious communities in many places gave attention to the environment. Activists urged us to take care of the places we inhabit and the wild places which are home to plants and animals. Some talked about the ethics of caring for the land, of respecting the land for itself, and of cultivating an attitude of gratitude to the land for the gifts of water and food and shelter which it provides. Many religious traditions, such as those of Aboriginal Australia described by Rose, assert that human beings have a responsibility to care for the earth.[24] At the same time, the ecological crises of our time make it clear that we have lacked forethought or have let the incentive of profits deflect us from that responsibility.[25] Local environmental struggles to protect places valued by communities as part of their habitat and history reflect how keenly people may feel the relationship to place. Contemporary environmental movement organizations (EMOs), some with religious motivations, are seeking, through networking, to engage the vitality of local struggles in common efforts to influence the actions of governments and companies.[26]

CONCLUSION

Place remains an underdeveloped concept in religious studies. Yet the papers collected in this volume point to important possibilities that attention to place offers for the study of religion. We tend to examine beliefs and ritual practice with reference to historical and social circumstances, but with little reference to their embeddedness in particular physical environments. Over twenty years ago Michel Foucault appealed for a social theory that takes place and space seriously.[27] It is time now to press for the development of approaches in the study of religion that take place seriously and examine the intersection of geographical place, social place, and sacred place. An interrogation of the concepts we use in the study of religion suggests that we need to expand our repertoire and that place is an effective concept for examining important aspects of religious traditions. As the lectures demonstrate, human beings and the natural world are inextricably entwined in particular locations. As biological beings we occupy space and as cultural beings, engaged in various forms of religion, we transform it into place.

NOTES

1. Among works that discuss perceptions of place are: John A. Agnew and James S. Duncan, eds., *The Power of Place: Bringing Together Geographical and Sociological Imagination* (Boston: Unwin Hyman, 1989); Steven Feld and Keith H. Basso, eds., *Senses of Place* (Santa Fe, N.M.: School of American Research Press, 1996); Eric Hirsch and Michael O'Hanlon, eds., *The Anthropology of Landscape* (Oxford: Clarendon Press, 1995); Peter Jackson and Jan Penrose, eds., *Constructions of Race, Place, and Nation* (London: UCL Press, 1993); Simon Schama, *Landscape and Memory* (New York: Knopf, 1995); Yi-Fu Tuan, *Passing Strange and Wonderful: Aesthetics, Nature, and Culture* (Washington, D.C.: Island Press/Shearwater Books, 1993), and his earlier work *Topophilia: A Study of Environmental Perception, Attitudes, and Values* (Englewood Cliffs, N.J.: Prentice-Hall, 1974).

2. The lecturer whose presentation is not included here was anthropologist and musicologist Steven Feld. His topic, "Place of Spirits and Spirits of Place in a New Guinea Rainforest," was presented with slides and music as well as text. Feld's important work on the place and culture of the Bosavi people of the Southern Highlands of Papua New Guinea includes articles, books, and several CDs. Among them are: Steven Feld, "Waterfalls of Song: An Accoustemology of Place Resounding in Bosavi, Papua New Guinea," in Steven Feld and Keith H. Basso, eds., *Senses of Place* (Santa Fe, N.M.: School of American Research Press, 1996); *Sound and Sentiment: Birds, Weeping, Poetics, and Song in Kaluli Expression* (Philadelphia: University of Pennsylvania Press, 1990); *Voices of the Rainforest: A Day in the Life of the Kaluli People* (Rykodisc, 1990); *Bosavi: Rainforest Music from Papua New Guinea*, recorded and annotated by Steven Feld (Smithsonian Folkways Recordings and the Institute of Papua New Guinea Studies, 2001).

3. Allan Pred, *Places, Practice and Structure: Social and Spatial Transformation in Southern Sweden, 1750–1850* (Cambridge: Polity Press, 1984).

4. Anne Buttimer, "Home, Reach, and the Sense of Place," in Anne Buttimer and David Seamon, eds., *The Human Experience of Space and Place* (New York: St. Martin's Press, 1980), 170.

5. David Welchman Gegeo, "Cultural Rupture and Indigeneity: The Challenge of (Re)visioning 'Place' in the Pacific," *The Contemporary Pacific* 13, no. 2 (fall 2001): 493–94. The two articles referred to in parentheses in the quotation are: Karen Ann Watson-Gegeo and David Welchman Gegeo, "Shaping the Mind and Straightening out Conflicts: The Discourse of Kwara'ae Family Counseling," in *Disentangling Conflict Discourse in Pacific Societies*, ed. Karen Ann Watson-Gegeo and Geoffrey M. White, 161–213 (Stanford, Calif.: Stanford University Press, 1990); and Karen Ann Watson-Gegeo and David Welchman Gegeo, "The Impact of Church Affiliation on Language Use in Kwara'ae (Solomon Islands)," *Language*

in Society 20, no. 4 (1991): 533–55. For further discussion of ways in which the languages of space and time condense in a Melanesian society, see also Margaret Jolly, "Another Time, Another Place," *Oceania* 69, no. 4 (1999): 282–99.

6. Gegeo, "Cultural Rupture and Indigeneity," 498.

7. Folk songs are full of nostalgia for remembered or misremembered places. For example, the line from the John Denver song, "Country Road, take me home to the place I belong," evokes nostalgia for a place where we can be in harmony with our surroundings and with other people. The singer evokes a longing for a rural place of a bygone era, for an America which is part reality and part imagination. Similarly, Irish immigrants or the children of immigrants may transport themselves back to a remembered or imagined Old Country through the singing of "Galway Bay" or "The Rose of Tralee."

8. Gaston Bachelard, *The Poetics of Space* (Boston: Beacon Press, 1964).

9. Richard Eves, "Seating the Place: Tropes of Body, Movement and Space for the People of Lelet Plateau, New Ireland (Papua New Guinea)," in James J. Fox, ed., *The Poetic Power of Place: Comparative Perspectives on Austronesian Ideas of Locality* (Canberra: Australian National University, 1997), 174.

10. See, for example, Mircea Eliade, *The Sacred and the Profane: The Nature of Religion*, trans. Willard Trask (New York: Harper and Row, 1955).

11. Ibid., 10.

12. Ibid., 21.

13. Rudolf Otto, *The Idea of the Holy* (London: Oxford University Press, 1923).

14. Both Otto and Eliade have been criticized for a tendency to privilege Western perspectives on religion. In speaking of the Holy and the sacred they assume the existence of a universal phenomenon, a structure of reality, which, they claim, is variously manifested in different cultures and in different places. Their expressions seem to be more invested with the God of the Western traditions than is appropriate for terms intended to be used cross-culturally. Traditions which posit a multiplicity of powers and beings which interact with the human community might not be most accurately portrayed by subsuming them under the rubric of the Holy or the sacred. However, the language of religious studies, like any other language, shifts and develops, and it seems that many who employ the notion of the sacred construe it more widely than Eliade might have first intended.

15. Lindsay Jones, *The Hermeneutics of Sacred Architecture: Experience, Interpretation, Comparison*, Volume Two, *Hermeneutical Calisthenics*, Religions of the World (Cambridge, Mass.: Center for the Study of World Religions, Harvard Divinity School, 2000), xiii.

16. Jonathan Z. Smith, *Map Is Not Territory* (Leiden: E. J. Brill, 1978), 101.

17. Ibid., 291, 309.

18. Mikhail M. Bakhtin, "Forms of Time and of the Chronotope in the Novel," in *The Dialogic Imagination: Four Essays*, ed. Michael Holquist, trans. Caryl Emerson and Michael Holquist (Austin: University of Texas Press, 1981).

19. Ibid., 85.

20. For a description of the *ceque* system, see Brian S. Bauer, *The Sacred Landscape of the Inca: The Cusco Ceque System* (Austin: University of Texas Press, 1998).

21. Philip Arnold, Eating Landscape: Aztec and European Occupation of Tlalocan (Boulder: University of Colorado Press, 1999).

22. Ibid., 245.

23. In contrast to the attitude of Hildegard and her community, that music can be part of an experience of heaven, some religious traditions have seen music, particularly instrumental music, as distracting and dangerous, a tool of evil.

24. "The Care of the Earth" is the title of a sermon given by Joseph Sittler (1904–1987). A Lutheran pastor and professor of theology in the Divinity School at the University of Chicago, Sittler was among a handful of scholars and pastors in the 1940s and 1950s who addressed environmental degradation as a religious isssue. The sermon can be found in Joseph Sittler, *The Care of the Earth and Other University Sermons* (Philadelphia: Fortress Press, 1964), and is reprinted along with other writings by Sittler on ecology and religion in Steven Bouma-Prediger and Peter Bakken, eds, *Evocations of Grace: The Writings of Joseph Sittler on Ecology, Theology, and Ethics* (Grand Rapids, Mich.: W. B. Eerdmans, 2000).

25. See, for example, the several volumes in the CSWR series "Religions of the World and Ecology" (Cambridge, Mass.: Center for the Study of World Religions, Harvard Divinity School, 1997–).

26. For a set of essays addressing the relationship of local and global in environmental efforts, see Christopher Rootes, ed., *Environmental Movements: Local, National, and Global* (London and Portland, Oreg.: Frank Cass, 1999).

27. Michel Foucault, *Power/Knowledge* (Brighton, Sussex: Harvester Press, 1980), 149.

OWL DUNE TALES: DIVINE POLITICS AND DESERTED PLACES IN RAJASTHAN

ANN GRODZINS GOLD

INTRODUCTION

I was initially gripped by the vitality of arid Rajasthan's richly storied landscapes while studying pilgrimage for my dissertation research, about two decades ago. Narratives imbued terrain seemingly devoid of charm with value, beauty, and power – evoking reverence. I recall scrambling up a barren rocky slope behind my eager companions to be shown what seemed the faintest scratch on its unyielding surface, an indentation I would never have noticed were it not marked by former pilgrims' worshipful vermilion. This was the hoofprint of a deity's horse, its divine vision a testimony to mythic reality and a blessing to travelers. The horse's passage across this terrain was part of an epic plot, thus mapped onto sacred geography, as well as painted on scrolls.[1]

Localized narratives of goddesses and gods, as I encountered them in Rajasthan, were more than imaginative embellishments on hard geophysical reality. It seemed rather that landscapes, inhabitants, and oral tales existed in relationships of mutual construction. To use the language of history of religions, not only were places chartered as hierophanous by stories, but new stories – relating and perpetuating hierophanies – were generated by places, set in motion as devotees interacted with resident divinities.[2] Pilgrims carried home mud from a murky pond where God once bathed, or ash from offering lamps, or flowers from an altar to be ingested as cure or treasured as talismans. Persons soliciting or celebrating a miraculous power's beneficence in their lives would mark transactions of grace and gratitude in ways that affected a shrine's physical appearance. For example, some tied strings or cloth strips to branches or pillars in symbolic transference of affliction to the deity's neutralizing power; some hung "cradle baskets" from trees in thanks for the birth of a child; some decorated old and constructed new buildings to celebrate all kinds of wishes come true.

Deities appeared to possess effective agency, to be actors in their own stories. If an oblivious or greedy woodcutter hacked a tree limb within a shrine's boundaries, punishment only attributable to divine agency fell rapidly on the culprit and his family: stomach aches, fainting spells, fire. Tales of divine protection of places, sustaining an ecologically benign loveliness, were an initial focus for me as I sought to understand links between religion and environment.[3] However, these were limited cases.

Eventually, I attempted to expand my comprehension of the physical engagement of religious stories and rituals with earthly localities beyond the limits of bounded sacred places. My starting point was the barren hillsides, offering stark contrast with lush sacred groves. I pursued morally laden narratives of deforestation, and thus was led by Rajasthani farmers and herders to history, through memories.[4]

With this essay I return in a fashion to my original interest in special places imbued by narrative with meanings and virtual powers – performative powers, affecting powers. But I shall not call this return full circle, for several reasons. Chief among these is a shift of primary focus – from verdant, protected, popular shrines to a desolate and deserted place. The Owl Dune is hardly a pilgrimage magnet; neither, however, is it ordinary, or profane. Owl Dune tales, fragments of local history, have to do with a village that was wiped out, depopulated, and buried in sand. The foundations of houses and at least one shrine are still visible there. Stories about these remains, together with another set of place tales I shall consider in this essay, deal not only with protection but with destruction; not only with devotion but with resistance, flight, and fission. It is not for nothing that my title contains the word "politics."

About ten years of studying rural history has taught me much about the power struggles and oppressions of the not-so-remote past. I easily detect their imprint (or is it their shadow?) in tales of divine power – certainly more visible than a mare's hoofprint on rocky terrain. In suggesting that sacred places may embody or bear witness to political stories, I do not intend to treat religious experiences of place reductively. Rather, I am interested in the ways religious realities interact with political ones in mutually transformative fashion.[5]

Akhil Gupta and James Ferguson have suggested that anthropologists need to turn toward "a focus on social and political processes of place making," and – following Liisa Malkki – that it is wrong to take as normal or natural "the rootedness of peoples and cultures in 'their own' territories."[6] Malkki herself states that "There has emerged a new awareness of the global social fact that, now more than perhaps ever before, people are chronically mobile and routinely displaced. . . ." However, she argues that ideas about rootedness have falsely infused social theory, blinding it to past motion. Thus Malkki believes that although today mobility is granted "more analytic visibility," it has always existed.[7]

Rajasthani villagers in both historical accounts and imaginative place tales keep the possibility of migrations and disappearances of peoples well in mind. This theme recurred persistently – and, to me at the time,

Fig. 1. Ruins in the Owl Dune (Photo: Ann Grodzins Gold)

inexplicably – in two epic tales of renouncer-kings which absorbed my scholarly energies a number of years ago. In these tales, not only are some cities founded in the wilderness, but others are emptied until "only owls hooting" remain (although they may eventually be resettled by magic or grace).[8] The owl's inauspicious voice conventionally signals the collapse of ruling power and subsequent desolation.[9] I shall briefly allude in concluding to those legendary migrations. However, most of this chapter examines two oral historical accounts of real places associated with peoples in motion.

Philip Arnold in his recent provocative book on Aztecs, *Eating Landscape*, argues for defining "place" as "direct negotiation of material life," in contrast to "space" as "constructed from the imagination." Arnold wishes to view religion as "formed by the human interaction with an exterior material world." The religion that interests him is fundamentally locative, and thus has everything to do with place. In this it differs from utopian or "nowhere" religions.[10] I am convinced that Hinduism spans, and thus diffuses, any firm locative/utopian distinction (even as it is perpetually and fundamentally both textual and oral tradition–based). Nonetheless, I find that much of rural Rajasthan's religious life is literally grounded in places. Imagination flourishes in the stories to come, but their mythopoetics reside in geophysical landscapes, negotiating them materially (to follow Arnold's phrasing).

Edward Casey (a philosopher who talks with anthropologists) offers a helpful formulation in his essay neatly titled, "How to Get from Space to Place in a Fairly Short Stretch of Time." Casey writes:

> . . . the eventful potency of places includes their cultural specificity. Time and history, the diachronic media of culture, are so deeply inscribed in places as to be inseparable from them – as inseparable as the bodies that sustain these same places and carry the culture located in them.[11]

Casey's words evoke in capsule form what I would like to achieve here: that is, to realize the "eventful potency" of a few Rajasthani spots. This potency is an attribute of memory, recreated in tellings of the past.[12]

The first tales I shall consider are of the Owl Dune, a ruined and deserted settlement adjoining the prosperous and lively village of Ghatiyali where I have been occasional resident and visiting anthropologist since 1979. The second tales – of two deities, a goddess and her male agent, Bhairuji – involve a complex story of human politics, collective action, and divine will. This goddess, called Ghāṇṭī kī Mātājī, originally resided in one spot with her attendant, Ḍhūṇḍā kā Bhairūjī; their powers were united and interdependent. However, the two divinities were irrevocably split apart when their prime worshipers, the Mauja Minas, made an abortive exodus from the local kingdom of Sawar.

Both accounts feature divine curses; but while the holy man's curse on the Owl Dune resulted in a sudden fatal cataclysm, the goddess's curse upon the Minas unfolded as slower and subtler processes of displacement. Over not much more than a century, she caused a community to dwindle from four hundred families to two and one-half. In concluding, I shall refer briefly to the Nath yogi epics in which we find related themes of demographic flux that may echo and comment on the historical tales that are my central concern.

THE OWL DUNE, THE CAVE, AND HANUMAN: RUINED PLACES AND ENDURING POWERS

Field diary, 7 February 1993: Bhoju and I walked to the Owl Dune where the buried city is said to be; where Gopi, maybe using the power of his magic armband, obtained silver coins but Sukh Devji and Narayan Gujar went mad; where on festival nights the mysterious lights flicker.

On a desolate sandy rise known as *ghūgh thaḷā*, or "Owl Dune," lie the ruins of an ancient settlement that, I was told, predated Ghatiyali. The Owl Dune is not exactly a sacred place; neither is it ordinary, or profane. As a ruin, it evokes more fear than reverence; in its sandy space lie not only scattered shards of myth and history, but lingering spirits. In Ghatiyali, the spirits of deceased persons may become benign deities when they are identified, enshrined, and appropriately served by living persons. By contrast, unknown spirits are potentially threatening; whatever nameless souls linger in the Owl Dune would be untended, needy, and frightening.[13]

Fig. 2. The sandy Owl Dune foregrounded (Photo: Ann Grodzins Gold)

Buried in sand, the Owl Dune remains a ghost-ridden, sub-rosa reality, one my collaborator, Bhoju Ram Gujar, and I found difficult to uncover. It is a place where, as evoked in my 1993 diary citation noted above, a few fearless eccentrics and magicians still occasionally seek buried treasure. Some even claim to have found it, but like most spellbound riches, those yielded by the Owl Dune prove easier to hoard than to enjoy.

The former settlement had been wiped out, I had vaguely heard over the years, by some kind of natural, supernatural, or magically induced natural disaster. Some said a sandstorm, others, an earthquake. Again according to general talk, the place had been a "thieves' village." I was led to conclude – without much investigation – that its destruction was posed as some kind of Old Testament–like divine retribution visited on a sinful people.

When my research took its historical turn, I readily tracked the larger political history of the twenty-seven-village kingdom of Sawar, where Ghatiyali is located, back through lineages of Rajput princes. These trace their genealogical descent to the important kingdom of Udaipur, and their political descent, in terms of control over land, to a seventeenth-century grant from the Mughal emperor Jahangir. But the Owl Dune's past, undated, seemed to have nothing at all to do with the nobility and its machinations. Fragmentary accounts I was able to glean centered on Minas, former "tribals" now well settled in the area as farmers.[14] Before the advent of Rajputs, it was commonly said, Minas were the dominant group in this region – but that was more than a thousand years ago by anyone's rough reckoning.

Minas are known by caste stereotyping as a fierce community: sometimes desperadoes from whom farmers and kings equally required protection; sometimes guards in the service of kings, ensuring safe passage. Doubtless they operated in both modes, and perhaps more commonly in neither.[15] However, this whole region was historically associated with activities of thieves. Local geography has place names like "Thieves' Valley," and multiple stories of past environmental lushness stressed equally travelers' perils from predatory beasts and humans. Minas have been settled and more or less law-abiding for a few generations, but other communities, like the caste called Sansi, retired from lives of highway robbery only recently. We interviewed a Sansi reform leader who described his community sharing loot with Rajput rulers in the years immediately preceding Independence.

In 1997 Bhoju Ram Gujar and I made an effort to gather what information we could on pre-Rajput or non-Rajput local history. In Mori, a village off the main road and dominated by Minas, Bhairu Mauja Mina gave us one fragment about the Owl Dune. He told Bhoju and me that the ruined houses still visible there had belonged to bandits (*dākū*) living in hamlets in the jungle. He did not specify Mina bandits. Bhairu told us the following story of the bandits' bad end, in which he introduced a figure well known from Ghatiyali's religious history, the Gufāwālā Bābā, or "Holy Man of the Cave," shortened here (as in earlier publications) to "the Cave Baba." The Cave Baba was an ascetic whose shrine, on one hillside, is an important site in the local sacred landscape, associated with protection from natural disasters.[16] Bhairu said:

> The Cave Baba finished them [the bandits] off. Once he was sitting doing ascetic practice [*tapasyā*]; and his disciples went on begging rounds but they didn't receive any food in the whole settlement [*kherā*]: Kapuri Washerwoman, Gangali Oil-presser, no one gave them any alms. . . .[17]

Then the guru came out of his meditation trance. His women disciples were bathing, and he noticed they had marks on their heads [from carrying heavy burdens of firewood].

They told him, "In this settlement, no one ever gives us alms and so we have been collecting wood and selling it in order to feed you."

The guru told them to warn all the people, "Leave this area before tomorrow morning. Cross the Banas River."

So the disciples told the people, "The guruji is angry," and some left. Those who didn't leave were swallowed up, destroyed: the earth turned over [*prithvī palaṭ gayī*; an earthquake], and everything was finished.

Then the guru left Kāṇṭolā [the dense wooded hillside] and the cave.[18] As he was leaving, his clothes stuck in the *dhokaṛā* trees and he cursed the jungle, "Your wood will never be straight!"[19] So from that day, if you wander through all of Kāṇṭolā, you cannot find any straight wood.

Sometimes [in the Owl Dune] you find old things, wealth, remnants of houses, but it was all finished off at that time. And Sawar [as we know it today] was settled later.

This story, fragment though it is, is evocative. I was initially fascinated by its geographic and environmental motifs, which include the past abundance of valued *dhokaṛā* trees (much diminished today), and a just-so story about their awkward, not aesthetically pleasing forms. The Banas River is a kind of imprecise boundary for the kingdom of Sawar, which in the era of this story has not yet been established. Here the river becomes a boundary for that terrain subjected to the guru's wrath, suggesting that the whole kingdom of Sawar developed over cursed ruins. We might speculate that this is a Mina interpretation of Rajput encroachment.

There is indeed a religious causality attributed to the disastrous end of the settlement, but its moral is not as straightforward as I had initially assumed would be the case with a "thieves' village." Something else is going on here. The old inhabitants were bandits, but that is explicitly not why they were doomed. Had they been generous bandits, alms-giving bandits, god-fearing bandits who paid generous respect to holy men and women, they might have survived.

It strikes me that the relationship posed here between ascetics and

Fig. 3. Portrait of Bhairu Mauja Mina (Photo: Ann Grodzins Gold)

worldly folks (in this case, thieves) parallels a relationship between wild places and settled places which various Indologists have explored in textual sources. Householders' well-being is removed from, but fundamentally linked to, renouncers' existence, and a necessary exchange relationship is often assumed between these two kinds of people. Similarly, royal or urban or worldly power is removed from but fundamentally linked to flourishing wildness. Give-and-take between settlement and jungle is necessary for the perpetuation of life.[20] Renouncers live in the jungle and seem to possess some control over the powers of nature. So the two apparently necessary but danger-fraught interdependencies – of kingdoms and forests, and of householders and renouncers – are themselves interlocked. Should any of these precarious balances be broken, disaster results.[21]

Sitting in front of Ghatiyali's Mataji Temple with Ganga Ram Mina and Shri Kishan Regar, we gathered another bit of Mina history, glorifying the heroic bandits who dwelled in the Owl Dune. Bhoju had asked who had "ruled" in Ghatiyali before the Rajputs, and Ganga Ram told us that a certain lineage had lived here in the "place where the sand is." He explicitly identified the bandits as Mina, and told us something we had not heard from others: they were "the ones who installed Balaji."

Fig. 4. Kāṇṭolā (the thorny hillside), looking up toward the cave
(Photo: Ann Grodzins Gold)

In Rajasthan, Balaji is the most common name for Hanuman – the heroic and divine monkey devotee of Lord Ram in the popular *Ramayana* epic. Ganga Ram refers to a shrine called alternatively Kāntolā kā Bālājī (Balaji of the Thorny Hill) or more commonly Jhāṁṇṭhā kā Bālājī. The latter means, literally, "Balaji of the Pubic Hairs" and is another linguistic recollection of the environmental past; the trees in this area, crooked though they may have been, were once as thickly set as curly pubic hairs.

Ganga Ram described the forefather of these Mina worshipers of Hanuman as "a man, or a thief, a criminal. And nobody knew what his caste was; he came here and said, 'I am a Mina.' He married a Mina in Mori village and he is the person who settled this area; from his genera-tion came the Minas of Ghatiyali. . . ." So this original settler was not only criminal but casteless. This says something about the arbitrary and fluid nature of caste identity in ancient, "lawless" or stateless times. To claim identity, at least for a desperado, was to possess it.[22]

The only other information Ganga Ram divulged was that this founder bandit had once stolen "the entire Gangaur with all its ornaments" from Jaipur, and brought them back here – to Ghatiyali. In the major princely state of Jaipur, the festival of Gangaur occasions a magnificent proces-sion honoring the goddess Parvati. This performative display of power and grandeur was integral to Jaipur state's identity. Such a deed escalates the buried village's criminal history to heroic status.[23]

Another old man, a gardener, told us a totally unrelated tale about the first inhabitants of Ghatiyali. His was a calm and stylized tale, almost like a creation myth, in which the great deities Shiva and Parvati are the main actors, setting caste forefathers upon the earth. I shall not relate the tale here, but I will note that it has one thing in common with those we have just considered: it asserts that the Mina community was present from earliest times. Moreover, the tale claims that three other original castes who lived in this place – Brahmins, Gujars, and Malis – used to say "Ram Ram" to the Minas at the important festivals of Holi and Divali (as in later times all caste communities would respectfully greet the Rajput rulers on holidays). In other words, this mythic origin story asserts that Minas in remote, foundational eras had superior social status, were in-deed the dominant, central caste. Rajputs, explicitly defined as non-indigenous, thoroughly usurped authority later in history.[24]

Let me attempt to pull together a few significant elements garnered from the skimpy Owl Dune tales. On the one hand, the area's earliest citizenry are identified not only as criminals, but as heedless of all dharma or morality, refusing to honor ascetics, and looting religious performances. They were bold, but rash. On the other hand, the bandits' legacy to Ghatiyali turns out to be not only the spooky buried city of the Owl Dune with its elusive and dangerous treasures and its lesson of retribution, but the still active and beneficent shrine of Balaji.

To characterize the unfortunate early residents simply as amoral bandits who were appropriately destroyed does not jibe with their having established the shrine of Hanuman, an important place of protection and assistance. Then, there is the cave, strongly associated with renouncers'

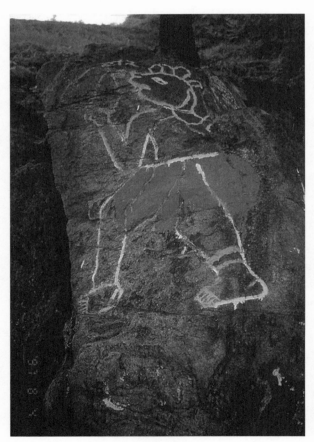

Fig. 5. Image of Balaji (Hanuman) painted on a rock, marking the path to his shrine (Photo: Ann Grodzins Gold)

power, a place both frightening and beneficent, even today. Might the power of the cave, associated with renouncers, and that of Hanuman, associated with the victorious bandits, have been in some kind of rivalry? I do not know, but the stories are suggestive.

The cave, too, had deteriorated over the years, if not quite to ruin. It was restored, around the 1960s, by a living renouncer, Marya Maharaj (a former Gujar resident of the village), who was reputed to have performed significant miracles by the Cave Baba's grace. In modern times, villagers may pay respect to both shrines or to neither, as they seek help with life needs or crises, according largely to personal devotional inclinations.

The triangulated powers of the cave, the Hanuman temple and the buried village in the Owl Dune do have some converging moral commentaries and impact. The tales suggest, among other things, that the goods of life must be shared for society and nature to prosper safely; and that the line between rulers and bandits is a very fine one. They show that ascetically generated power may concentrate in one place, like the cave, but its force when effectively wielded emanates throughout a region. Such places are not eternal sites of immanent power in the fashion of pan-Hindu pilgrimage centers chartered in the Sanskrit *Puranas* as sin-removing, such as Pushkar Lake or any sacred city on the Ganges River. Rather, they are sites of overflowing narrative potency, storied places where the agency and actions of human and divine beings have generated meanings at once historical and religious, contingent but enduring.

ḌHŪṆḌĀ KĀ BHAIRŪJĪ / GHĀṆṬĪ KĪ MĀTĀJĪ: FISSION AND AGENCY

This second tale of place and displacement also involves the Mina community and a curse. It shows the Minas, about a thousand years later in narrative time, severely disadvantaged and under the harsh rule of immigrant Rajputs who had by then assumed total dominance. In its greater historical immediacy, the political negotiations embedded in this tale are both less remote and less obscure.

I had learned during my first fieldwork period in 1980 about a goddess (Mataji) who had left Ghatiyali when her people decided to emigrate, but who refused to return when they themselves returned. Her Bhairuji, however, had stayed behind. The Bhairuji in question, Ḍhūṇḍā kā

Bhairūjī, happened to be the shrine closest to my first dwelling in Ghatiyali. Although every goddess shrine had a Bhairuji associated with it, not every Bhairu in the village was located near a goddess; some were independent from the beginning.[25] Hence, I might not have marked this Bhairu's isolation, had I not by chance heard the tale of the goddess who split from him – while I was walking down the road past her place together with talkative companions. Not until many years later, while tracking local history, did I came to learn why the Minas had moved their goddess down the road in the first place. The reason was a dispute with the local king over a single acacia (*deśī bambūl*) tree.

Once again, Bhoju and I hoped to tap Ganga Ram Mina's extensive oral historical and religious knowledge, but it was another old man, Shri Kishan, a leather-worker (Regar), who filled in the details on the story I came to think of as the "Minas' aborted Exodus." I do not know why Ganga Ram, usually talkative, allowed Shri Kishan the main voice in telling his goddess's story. Perhaps the Minas are not at all proud of this incident, of which the denouement is their double subjection – first to the king and then to the goddess's curse of a dwindling community.

Ganga Ram himself informed us that there were once three hundred and fifty houses in Ghatiyali belonging to the Mauja Mina lineage, while today there were only two and one-half (the half being a family with no progeny). Shri Kishan Regar then began the tale:

Shri Kishan: They are cursed by this Mataji [goddess]: Ghāṇṭī kī Mātājī. [This name might translate literally as "Valley Mother," but is understood to mean the "Mother from Ghatiyali." Ghatiyali's name, in fact, refers to its geophysical setting, on low land nestled among hills.]

Bhoju: Why did they leave Ghatiyali?

Ganga Ram: In previous times, the Mina had a fight with the Court [the ruler of the twenty-seven-village kingdom of which Ghatiyali was the second most populous settlement], and that's why they left.

Bhoju: Why, what was the fight about?

Shri Kishan: One time some Mina people had cut an acacia (*bambūl*) that was growing in their own field. And the king's manager caught them and rebuked them, "Why did you cut the *bambūl*? You will have to be fined!"

But they said, "We need shutters and plows! How can we pay fines for all the wood that we use? If we can't cut wood from our own fields, from where will we cut it?"

For this reason, they got into a fight. Then, the king's men took the *bambūl* they had cut into the fort; they took it away from the Mina. . . . And so they left, because of the *bambūl* tree.

You know the shrine – Ḍhūṇḍā kā Bhairūjī. Previously both the goddess and Bhairuji were there. The Minas wanted to take both deities along with them, but Bhairuji refused to go.

Bhoju: What do you mean, he "refused" to go?

Shri Kishan: They tried to dig it [the stone icon] out from the ground, but they were not successful; they were unable to do it. So they took Mataji, and still Bhairuji remains here.

When the goddess's *bhāv* came [that is, when the shrine priest became possessed by the goddess], she said, "You will return, but I will not return," and the Mina replied, "No, we will not return."[26]

When they were ready to leave, with all their things packed, a rider went to Sawar to inform the Court that the Mina were angry and ready to leave the kingdom. At this time the king was Madhav Singh. He convinced them to return.[27] So after that, they did come back, because the Court called them back. But the goddess would not come back with them, and she cursed the Minas: "Your lineage will not remain in Ghatiyali."

So from 350 houses, today there remain only two and one-half. Because of the goddess's curse. . . . And she stayed there.

Soon after that, Minas started leaving Ghatiyali, and they settled in Mori, Vajta, Napa ka Khera . . . [nearby villages].

Sometimes one, sometimes two families left at a time. All around this area, the houses of Mauja Minas are people who left Ghatiyali [following the curse].

In 1980 I had surveyed all the village shrines, assembling the results in a large binder. There I found this notation on Ḍhūṇḍā kā Bhairūjī: "When a ghost or witch comes, the *bhāv* is called [to facilitate exorcism]; it used to come to Bhoma Mauja Mina; after his death it comes to no one; the *nejā* [flag] of Navaratra stops here."

These two points are both significant. The shrine is treated during the festival of the goddess's nine nights as if she were still there, in spite of her icon's physical removal. Equally striking, as if confirming the curse, after the Mauja Mina shrine priest's death, there was no successor available to act as medium for what was essentially a lineage deity.

Reflecting back on this story after I completed a manuscript recording the bitter resentment by farmers of the former rulers' control over every product of the land, including trees, I easily reread it with messages of resistance: the Minas betrayed their community and deity by weakening in their original resolution. The goddess predicted their capitulation and disapproved of it. Presumably, the Court had pacified them and even returned their wood. But this small victory was not glorified, not even made explicit. And in accepting the Court's terms – most significantly – they broke a promise to their goddess. She, whose power is superior to the Court's, determines that Ghatiyali is no longer to be her proper place, or theirs. She makes their threat and defiance come true, even when they themselves have settled on compromise. Power struggles and tensions are at work on multiple dimensions here: the Minas and the Court, the goddess and her worshipers; even Bhairu and the goddess.

In today's local exegesis, I must acknowledge, this story has never been

Fig. 6. Ḍhūṇḍā kā Bhairūjī's shrine (Photo: Ann Grodzins Gold)

presented to me as a political tale. The tree protest origin of the whole episode tends to drop out of casual place lore. Rather, it is told as a story about Mataji's *līlā*, or divine play, and the chief moral seems to be that one may not uproot a goddess lightly.[28] Humans may vacillate, but not she; and her indulgence of human frailty is limited. The goddess did not, of course, withdraw her grace more than a few kilometers, and her shrine remains very popular today as a local healing site. Thus, she flourishes in her new place, but the Mauja Minas have dwindled without her in the village that was once home to them all.

Resorting to protest flight by the disempowered was a recognized political strategy in other parts of rural India. Saurabh Dube, for example, writing of a different region, tells us that "Chamars, along with other day laborers and ploughmen, adopted the desertion of villages as a mode of resisting officeholders, landlords, and rich peasants. . . ." Dube adds, "We should not underestimate the difficulties involved in the strategy of flight." Nonetheless, he finds that "it offered poor ploughmen and farm servants a feasible way to resist and retain their bargaining power."[29]

In the case of the Mauja Minas, a proud remnant of a once chiefly community, the ultimate outcome is that, due to the king's injustice,

Fig. 7. Wall painting at the shrine of Ghāṇṭī kī Mātājī, showing the goddess flanked by manifestations of Bhairuji (Photo: Ann Grodzins Gold)

Ghatiyali as a place is depleted both of its original subjects and of an important deity. In their dispersion, Mauja Minas have resettled in boondock villages such as Mori, out of the way of the Court's direct surveillance. In such backwoods settings, as many other unrelated interviews suggest, people are far freer to cut trees and otherwise defy government edicts in various ways.

RUINS IN OUR MIDST

My central image in this chapter has been the Owl Dune, a ruin whose very name is evocative of inauspicious desolation. Nicholas Dirks has recently used ruin imagery as an extended metaphor for social theory at the turn of the century. Departing from some observations by Walter Benjamin, Dirks writes: "The ruin is the only connection between the wonders of the past and the degradation of the present. The ruin puts us in awe of the mystifications that made civilization magnificent in the first place. The ruin is culture, both its reality and its representation."[30] Here Dirks speaks unabashedly in Eurocentric mode, thinking doubtless of the Acropolis or the Colosseum. But Indian villagers, too, contemplate the ruins in their midst, as testimonies of an ancient past. Their thoughts are rather less awestruck, but the urge to draw historical connections is just as vital.

The legends of renouncer-kings Gopi Chand and Bharthari are well known throughout North India. As performed in the regional dialect by a bard from Ghatiyali, the tales display a recurrent theme of demographic flux. Twice in Bharthari's tale and once in Gopi Chand's, entire populaces are temporarily displaced. In each case these events are obviously connected with demonstrations of how a king is not only responsible for, but dependent on, his subjects.

Consider one comic episode in the first segment of King Bharthari's tale. A distraught potter decides to quit his city because his donkey is embarrassing him and endangering his life by braying loudly and demanding to marry a princess. (The vociferous beast is really a king cursed by his father to be born in a donkey's womb.) The potter's move precipitates that of the rest of the populace. Royal servants then inform the king of a major problem in his domain:

Grain-giver, over whom are you ruling here? Only owls are left here in the village, only owls hooting. The whole city is empty. Not even a child remains.

The reference to owls encodes desolation in this imaginary account of a depopulated city, just as owls characterize the ghost town bordering the bard's own village.

In Bharthari's story, the cause of depopulation is neither natural disaster nor magical curses, but popular protest. The events transpire much as was the case with the Minas' aborted exodus. For the king immediately asks his servants why the people have left, and "what was troubling them?" He then negotiates personally with his people, accedes to their wishes, and brings them back to the capital with him. Thus, his city and meaningful rule are restored. In each depopulation episode in the epics, a king is similarly called upon to act humbly in order to restore his rule's value and repopulate his city (presumably thereby banishing the owls).[31]

As a native of Ghatiyali, the bard may have drawn on his local knowledge – of the Owl Dune's desolation and the Minas' protest strategy – to describe a legendary king's predicament. But in comparing these legendary depopulations with the local oral history of the Owl Dune's ruins and the Mauja Minas' aborted exodus and ultimately dwindled numbers, we find not only reflective continuity, but divergence.

The main difference between the imagined and the historically grounded scenarios is in closure. Neither of the "real" stories ends with restoration of normalcy. The Owl Dune will never be repopulated, its inhabitants are obliterated. Ghatiyali's goddess remains a few kilometers from her village, perpetually but uncomfortably separated from her Bhairuji. Thus, these tales rooted in – generated by – real places are indeed (as Arnold would insist) engaged with materiality, teaching of historical events as much as of timeless truths. At the broadest level, the tales of the Owl Dune and the Minas' goddess reveal a potent and dynamic interplay of narrative, place, and power; of divine prescience and human striving; of ghostly ruins and ongoing, everyday lives.[32]

NOTES

Bhoju Ram Gujar was an indispensable collaborator in all research efforts. I am deeply grateful to him and to Fulbright, the American Institute of Indian Studies, the National Endowment for the Humanities, an independent federal agency, and the College of Arts and Sciences of Syracuse University for generous and crucial support.

1. The hoofprint was of the regional hero-god, Lord Dev Narayan's mare. For Dev Narayan's epic, see Joseph C. Miller, Jr., *The Twenty-four Brothers and Lord Devnārāyaṇ: The Story and Performance of a Folk Epic of Rajasthan, India* (Ann Arbor, Mich.: UMI Dissertation Services, 1994).

2. A classic treatment of hierophanies in space would be Mircea Eliade, *The Sacred and the Profane*, trans. Willard R. Trask (New York: Harcourt, Brace, 1959).

3. See Ann Grodzins Gold and Bhoju Ram Gujar, "Of Gods, Trees, and Boundaries," *Asian Folklore Studies* 48 (1989): 211–29.

4. See Ann Grodzins Gold and Bhoju Ram Gujar, *In the Time of Trees and Sorrows: Nature, Power, and Memory in Rajasthan* (Durham, N.C.: Duke University Press, 2002).

5. On the politics of ritual in South Asian contexts, see, for example, Gyan Prakash, *Bonded Histories: Genealogies of Labour Servitude in Colonial India* (Cambridge: Cambridge University Press, 1990); see also Nicholas B. Dirks, "Ritual and Resistance: Subversion as a Social Fact," in *Contesting Power: Resistance and Everyday Social Relations in South Asia*, ed. Douglas Haynes and Gyan Prakash (Berkeley: University of California Press, 1992), 213–38.

6. Akhil Gupta and James Ferguson, "Culture, Power, Place: Ethnography at the End of an Era," in *Culture, Power, Place: Explorations in Critical Anthropology*, ed. Akhil Gupta and James Ferguson (Durham, N.C.: Duke University Press, 1997), 1–29, quote on pp. 6–7.

7. Liisa H. Malkki, "National Geographic: The Rooting of Peoples and the Territorialization of National Identity among Scholars and Refugees," in *Culture, Power, Place: Explorations in Critical Anthropology*, ed. Akhil Gupta and James Ferguson (Durham, N.C.: Duke University Press, 1997), 52–74, quote on p. 53.

8. Ann Grodzins Gold, *A Carnival of Parting* (Berkeley: University of California Press, 1992), 86, 254–55, 314–17.

9. That owls sign similar situations in the Hebrew Bible as well would suggest a zoological commonality observed in multiple traditions; thanks to Mary MacDonald for reminding me that Isaiah 34:8–15 and Psalm 102:6–7 associate owls with desolate and forsaken landscapes.

10. Philip P. Arnold, *Eating Landscape: Aztec and European Occupation of Tlalocan* (Niwot, Colo.: University Press of Colorado, 1999), 18. In his approach to religion and materiality, Arnold especially acknowledges the influence of Charles

Long, *Significations* (Philadelphia: Fortress Press, 1986). In his understandings of the locative nature of indigenous religions, Arnold builds from Jonathan Z. Smith, *Map Is Not Territory* (Leiden: E. J. Brill, 1978).

11. Edward S. Casey, "How to Get from Space to Place in a Fairly Short Stretch of Time: Phenomenological Prolegomena," in *Senses of Place*, ed. Steven Feld and Keith H. Basso (Santa Fe, N.M.: School of American Research Press, 1996), 13–52, quote on p. 44.

12. Edward S. Casey elucidates the mutual formation of landscape and memory in his *Remembering: A Phenomenological Study* (Bloomington: Indiana University Press, 1987). See also Ajay Skaria's brilliant treatment of wildness, memory, and history in his *Hybrid Histories: Forests, Frontiers, and Wildness in Western India* (Delhi: Oxford University Press, 1999); and, of course, Simon Schama, *Landscape and Memory* (New York, Vintage Books, 1995).

13. For an extensive discussion of lingering spirits of the dead in Ghatiyali, see Ann Grodzins Gold, *Fruitful Journeys: The Ways of Rajasthani Pilgrims* (Prospect Heights, Ill.: Waveland Press, 2000), 63–79.

14. For Minas, see Munshi Hardyal Singh, *The Castes of Marwar: Census Report of 1891* (Jodhpur: Books Treasure, 1990), 51–56. On the relations between Rajputs and other tribal peoples, Nandini Sinha's work on Bhils in Southern Rajasthan is illuminating; see her "State and the Tribe: A Study of the Bhils in the Historic Setting of Southern Rajasthan," *Social Science Probings*, March-December 1993, 55–67. For Udaipur District Bhils in modern times, including a helpful discussion of "Bhil-Rajput relations" both historical and contemporary, see Maxine Weisgrau, *Interpreting Development: Local Histories, Local Strategies* (Lanham, Md.: University Press of America, 1997).

15. Singh writes: "The Minas for generations were wholly given to robbery and general lawlessness, their national weapons being bows and arrows. From their very childhood they practised crime. . . ." He goes on to note that the "course of time has now refined the character of Minas, and they are more and more being persuaded to adopt peaceful habits." See his *Castes of Marwar*, 55–56. For an incisive critique of colonial uses of "criminality" applied to particular groups, see Shail Mayaram, "Criminality or Community? Alternative Constructions of the Mev Narrative of Darya Khan," *Contributions to Indian Sociology* 25 (1991): 57–84.

16. See Gold, *Fruitful Journeys*, 50–53.

17. These names of a powerful guru's female disciples, a washerwoman and an oil-presser woman, are standard legendary figures in North India and associated with Nath yogis; see Gold, *A Carnival of Parting*, 226–59.

18. Kāṇṭolā is the name of a large hill between Ghatiyali and Sawar where the cave and other shrines are located. One person glossed the name as "where there once was deep jungle." The term appears to derive from *kāṇṭo*, for thorn.

19. *Dhokaṛā* is Rajasthani for *Anogeissus pendula*, the dominant tree species in the Banas Basin before the severe deforestation that took place in the middle decades of the twentieth century.

20. See Nancy E. Falk, "Wilderness and Kingship in Ancient South Asia," *History of Religions* 13 (1973): 1–15, for kings and jungles in classical Hindu and Buddhist textual traditions. Further insights into these matters based on Sanskritic textual materials are found in J. C. Heesterman, *The Inner Conflict of Tradition* (Chicago: University of Chicago Press, 1985), 118, and Charles Malamoud, *Cuire le monde: Rite et pensée dans l'Inde Ancienne* (Paris: Editions La Decouverte, 1989), 93–114. For an interesting discussion of the relationship of kings to the jungle in a South Indian vernacular epic tradition, see Brenda E. F. Beck, *The Three Twins: The Telling of a South Indian Folk Epic* (Bloomington: Indiana University Press, 1982).

21. For additional discussion of these balances, see Ann Grodzins Gold, "Story, Ritual, and Environment in Rajasthan," in *Sacred Landscapes and Cultural Politics: Planting a Tree*, ed. Philip Arnold and Ann Grodzins Gold (Aldershot, Hampshire, Great Britain: Ashgate Publishing, 2001), 115–37.

22. Contrast this with an origin story I heard for the name Mina set in the mythic time when Parasurama – Vishnu's avatar – was pursuing his slaughter of Rajputs; those who were cowardly cried out, *maiṁ nahīṁ huṁ* ("I am not one"), which eventually contracted to Mina.

23. Elsewhere in Rajasthan, as described in Weisgrau, *Interpreting Development*, the Gavri drama still performed by Minas and Bhils in Udaipur District includes an episode in which the Jaipur Gangaur procession is attacked. It seems likely that the source of Ganga Ram Mina's tale lies in these still vital traditions. I might imaginatively speculate that the Minas offended the goddess in attacking her procession, but no one suggested this.

24. For dominant castes and ritual centrality, see Gloria Goodwin Raheja, *The Poison in the Gift* (Chicago: University of Chicago Press, 1988). I think it no accident that tropes of Mina dominance and Mina banditry are simultaneously current.

25. Bhairuji (Rajasthani for Bhairava) is a form or agent of Shiva, normally a presence at goddess shrines in this locality; see Gold, *Fruitful Journeys*. For Bhairava's larger identity in Shaivite myth, see David G. White, *Myths of the Dog-Man* (Chicago: University of Chicago Press, 1991), 102–6.

26. For oracular possession by deities, called *bhāv*, see Gold, *Fruitful Journeys*, 95, 154–86.

27. Madhav Singh was grandfather of Vansh Pradip Singh, the last pre-Independence ruler, who passed away in 1947. So this event probably takes place around the turn of the century.

28. Deities are often depicted as exercising agency over their shrines' locations. A well-known Rajasthani example is the story of cart wheels lodging in the mud near the unlikely setting of Nathdwara, when devotees were attempting to carry Shri Nathji – a form of Krishna – to Udaipur; for one version, see Amit Ambalal, *Krishna as Shrinathji* (New York: Mapin International, 1987), 52. Richard H. Davis discusses the ways late medieval narratives about icons asserted that "a special relationship linked the deity's image to its particular site, and that this connection resulted from divine choice rather than human initiative"; see his *Lives of Indian Images* (Princeton: Princeton University Press, 1997), 122–23.

29. Saurabh Dube, *Untouchable Pasts: Religion, Identity, and Power among a Central Indian Community, 1780–1950* (Albany: State University of New York Press, 1998), 32–33.

30. Nicholas B. Dirks, "In Near Ruins: Cultural Theory at the End of the Century," in *In Near Ruins: Cultural Theory at the End of the Century*, ed. Nicholas B. Dirks (Minneapolis: University of Minnesota Press, 1998), 1–18, quote on p. 10.

31. Gold, *Carnival of Parting.*

32. For place stories, I find much help in Keith H. Basso, "Wisdom Sits in Places: Notes on a Western Apache Landscape," in *Senses of Place*, ed. Steven Feld and Keith H. Basso (Santa Fe, N.M.: School of American Research Press, 1996), 53–90. See also Julie Cruikshank, *The Social Life of Stories: Narrative and Knowledge in the Yukon Territory* (Lincoln: University of Nebraska Press, 1998), on "negotiating with narrative."

FROM DAN TO BEER-SHEBA AND FROM THE WILDERNESS TO THE SEA: LITERAL AND LITERARY IMAGES OF THE PROMISED LAND IN THE BIBLE

NILI WAZANA

The Bible, a literary document, communicates perceptions of mental pictures molded in words. The task of deciphering their meaning is left to the readers. Lack of pictoral reflections of reality is most intensely felt in relation to descriptions of territories and their boundaries. Our modern conception of a land as a geographical entity, surrounded by well-defined borders, indicated by both physical marks and illustrated maps, naturally leads us to anticipate a clear notion of the dimensions of a specific land in the Bible. Where the modern scholar would insert a map to display territorial units – as current commentaries indeed often do – the text-based Bible employs more or less detailed literary descriptions of the land. It is therefore not surprising that readers have taken biblical descriptions pertaining to a land as literal guides for drawing maps, unaware that they may have been written in an altogether different mindset, pointing to important features other than its geographical dimensions.

In the present paper I propose that we regard images of the Promised Land in the Bible as literary descriptions; hence, the basis for examining them must begin with a literary analysis. Like all other biblical texts, they too are part of a charged ideological document, bearing religious notions and, sometimes, polemic undertones. I will offer a literary rather than a literal reading of the texts pertaining to geographical descriptions of the

Promised Land, which will point to the ideological and theological assumptions underlining them.

When interpreting literary images of Israel, it is imperative to note that the Land of Israel is not a distinct geographical unit today, nor has it been in the past, and it does not consist of a unified territory. It's natural borders are not easily defined. Although the Mediterranean Sea to the west and the Sinai Desert to the south can be reckoned as natural borders, definite circumscribing physical borders on the two remaining sides are harder to identify. It may be argued that the Jordan River could serve as a natural border to the East.[1] Although, as we shall see, it often did designate the eastern border in biblical conception, being a narrow, winding body of water, it was never called "river" (nahar) in the Bible, an appellation reserved for the big rivers of Egypt, Syria, and Mesopotamia.[2] The Jordan was never a definite obstacle to further settlements, natural conditions to the east of it similar to those to the west; and, in fact, more often than not, populations on both sides were ethnically and culturally linked, belonging to the same political unit. This being the case, the Syro-Arabian Desert formed the natural border, blocking settlement growth to the east.[3] Also, to the north there is no natural border. Although the Lebanon mountain range and its eastern parallel, the anti-Lebanon, are significant landmarks in themselves, their protuberant mountains rising to the height of 2,500 meters (about 8,300 feet) above sea level, they stretch from south to north, separated by a fertile valley, the Baqa'a, and at no point constitute any tangible natural barrier to expansion northward.

The Land of Israel is characterized by two main geographical features – the variety and diversity of its topography, climate, and plant and animal life in a relatively small area, and its configuration as a bridge between three continents, part of the larger civilized continuum that was the ancient Near East.[4] From a historical point of view, the events that shaped the history of this land were a manifestation of the interaction of those two factors, the meeting point of the forces from within and without. As a land of contrasts and conflicts, oscillating between external and internal forces, desert and cultivated area, unity and diversity, it is not surprising that this entity did not have a single set of political borders throughout its history. While its real borders changed shape as a result of

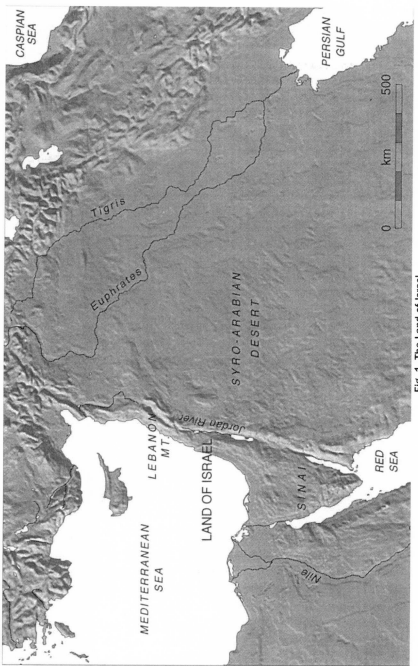

Fig. 1. The Land of Israel

changing circumstances, the concept of the extent of the Land also did not remain the same. The Bible testifies to the existence of different concepts of the extent of the Land of Israel, and these do not necessarily conform to any real set of borders. In this paper I will concentrate on images of one important concept pertaining to the Promised Land, as reflected in biblical texts relating to the formative period of the people of Israel.

THE TERRITORIAL CONCEPT OF THE PROMISED LAND

The first eleven chapters of the Pentateuch introduce the creation of the universe and development of world order, employing the word "land" (*'ereṣ*) in its most general meanings: "earth," "world" (e.g., Gen. 1:1–2); "dry land" opposed to "sea" (Gen. 1:10); or "humanity" – the dwellers of the earth (Gen. 6:11; 11:1). Accordingly, God's blessing to Adam, reiterated to Noah, is a divine commandment to "be fertile and increase and fill the earth (*ha-'areṣ*)" (Gen. 1:28; 9:1).[5] In these chapters the narrative sets the ground for the main and organizing theme of the majority of biblical writings – the relationship of the people of Israel with God, in which the Land of Israel plays a central role.[6] When Abraham enters the stage, marking the transition from a universalistic outlook to a nationalistic, Israelite one, his first divine message is an order to leave his native land (designated "your land, your native land") and to go to another, determined one: "the land (*ha-'areṣ*) that I will show you . . ." (Gen. 12:1). Although his destination remains unspecified, Abraham takes his family and sets out for "the land of Canaan" (verse 5), and it is from this point on that the articulate "land" (*ha-'areṣ*) stands as a recognized appellation for a specific area, assigned to Abraham's offspring: "The Lord appeared to Abram and said 'I will assign[7] this land to your offspring'" (Gen. 12:7).

At this point in the biblical narrative it is quite clear that the meaning of the term "land" is not the same as in the first eleven chapters of Genesis. Abraham is not promised the whole world. He is to leave his own land and to come as an outsider to another land, already in existence as a geographical unit and inhabited by a population which gave it its name: "The Canaanites were then in the land" (Gen. 12:6).

Clearly, the land alone was not all that God promised the patriarchs and their descendants. Together with inheritance of the land, he had designated for them numerous progeny combined with national greatness.[8]

These elements of the divine promise often appear together with the promise of the land, but they are neither identical nor inseparable. Thus, God promised Abraham that Ishmael, his son by Hagar, the Egyptian maid, shall be fertile and exceedingly numerous, applying in his case the same term used in the initial blessings to Abraham (Gen. 12:2) – "a great nation" (Gen. 17:20; 21:13, 18; cf. 16:9). At the same time it is obvious that Ishmael shall not inherit a land of his own. He will inhabit the desert, destined to "dwell alongside of all his kinsmen" (Gen. 16:12) and will be a nomad in the wilderness, occupying the steppes external to places of habitation. Ishmael, as Jon Levenson notes, while "falling within the promise to his father, will be 'a great nation' and 'a wild ass of a man,' but he falls, nonetheless, just outside the covenant of Abraham and shall not inherit the Promised Land."[9] Ishmael's destiny indicates that, of the two components of the promise, progeny and land, it is the latter that constitutes the special relationship – in other words, the covenant – between God and the chosen individuals in the book of Genesis, and later with their descendants, the people of Israel. The land grant is, therefore, the core and essence of the covenant, its defining component. It assumes even greater prominence according to Moshe Weinfeld's observation that the covenant with the patriarchs (with Abraham in particular) was structured on an unconditional royal land grant and not a bilateral treaty.[10] Accordingly, the land is not only one of the benefits awarded to the receptive partner, but the main issue of the covenant, its raison d'être.[11]

That the Promised Land is a whole and complete concept, separate from the people of Israel, is one of the central and unique themes of biblical ideology, enabling the community of Israel to exist apart from the land.[12] Yet it is remarkable that the first biblical mention of the Promised Land does not specify its extent or define its boundaries. Perhaps we can understand the obscure destination of the first imperative to Abraham (Gen. 12:1) as ancient Jewish tradition did, fitting it into the larger pattern of trials and obstacles through which God put him.[13] But when the promise is reiterated after Abraham arrives at his destination, we expect a more precise rendering of the limits of this consequential place than the general, offhand "this land" (Gen. 12:7).

The question of the definition of the Promised Land becomes even more intriguing since the language of the upcoming promises resonates with legal overtones, such as in the second divine promise, given on the occasion of the parting of Abram and his nephew Lot, when "the land" could not support them both:

> And the Lord said to Abram, after Lot had parted from him, "Raise your eyes and look out from where you are, to the north and south, to the east and west, for I give all the land that you see to you and your offspring forever. . . . Up, walk about the land, through its length and its breadth, for I give it to you. (Gen. 13:14–17)

Abraham is actively accepting the gift of land by traversing its length and breadth, reflecting most likely an ancient legal affirmation of the transfer of ownership.[14] Surveying the land (13:14–15) and lying on it (28:13)[15] also echo symbolic acts, validations of land acquisitions in ancient legal traditions.[16] Other phraseology apparent in the promise traditions suggests legal connotation as well, such as the technical use of *ntn* (assign)[17] and conveyance of the land for perpetuity.[18] Traces of appropriating land by pointing out the boundaries of the territory are also discernible in the final chapter of the book of Deuteronomy, when God, the owner, indicates the extent of the Promised Land to Moses (Deut. 34:1–4).[19] However, in the case of the promise of the land to the patriarchs, these quasi-legal allusions make use of terminology of land transfer, without actually delimiting the land in question. The language of the promise suffices, with general designations containing the definite article "(this) land" or, in the priestly terminology, "the land of Canaan," or "the land you sojourn in."[20] This kind of general expression is characteristic of the promise of the land in ten out of the eleven times that it is recorded.[21] The majority of the promise texts do not delineate, or even mention, the borders of this assigned territory.

The language of the texts suggests that the Promised Land was a conventional, well-known geographical unit, and the authors of these traditions were naturally referring to this concept every time they depicted it in the general terms "the/this land" or "the land of Canaan," just as the designation "Palestine" signifies essentially the territories comprising the biblical Israel and Judah in contemporary biblical studies.[22] Though the exact extent of the political-geographical unit may have fluctuated over the ages as a result of political and historical changes, the general designation is an accepted standard term referring to a known core area and adjacent peripheral zones. Can we nonetheless define the confines of the Promised Land alluded to in the patriarchal traditions?

The exact borders of the Promised Land were elucidated in great detail in the document attributed to P, entitled "The Land of Canaan with Its Various Boundaries" (Num. 34:1–12).[23] This is a verbal map, outlining the borders of the land of Canaan by a virtual tour following its four sides. Starting at the southeastern limit of the land, the description delineates the southern border from east to west, continuing clockwise to the western side, the north and the east, finally returning to the starting point, the Dead Sea (Num. 34:3–12). This precise description mentions around twenty separate geographical names, including settlements (i.e., Kadesh-barneʻa, Lebo-hamath), roads (the ascent of Akrabbim), mountains (Mount Hor), local rivers (Jordan), wadis (the Brook of Egypt), and seas (the Great Sea, the Sea of Galilee, the Dead Sea).[24] The priestly promise texts, which use the same appellation found in the comprehensive description – "the land of Canaan" – are thereby indicating that they are pertaining to the same, (elsewhere) well-defined territory. There is no way of telling whether the other sources, using the less specific but more obvious designation "this/the land" were also pointing to the same geographical concept or a different one. Numbers 34 is at any rate the only extensive description of the Promised Land in the traditions of the formative periods. Although we cannot rule out the possibility that the authors of these sources might have had a different extent in mind, they clearly indicate a specific, finite, known, and accepted concept of the Promised Land.

Our theory regarding the relationship of the promise traditions referring to the Promised Land without explicating her borders, and the document containing a detailed description of her borders, may find support in ancient Near Eastern political custom. Hittite diplomatic texts express a similar relationship between an explicit, precise delineation of a geographical region and a more general reference to it in political-legal contexts. Many Hittite vassal treaties delimit the borders of the vassal's realm; some do it in great detail. Sometimes, however, the Hittite king was satisfied with mention of a border description delineated in an earlier document, explaining why there was no need to depict these borders again: "My grandfather . . . wrote out the borders of the land of Amurru of his father, and gave it to him."[25] Further, many more Hittite diplomatic documents refer to specific geopolitical regions only by their names, without delimiting their borders or even relying on an earlier delineation, still expressing a Hittite interest in determining and keeping the territories of the subordinate countries.[26] Vassal treaties cited the borders of the region in question only when these were changed,[27] disputed,[28] or were emphasized for security and military purposes.[29] Otherwise, a general reference to the land in question sufficed.

The approach reflected in Hittite sources clarifies why the majority of the promise texts do not define the extent of the land. Analogous to the political-diplomatic sphere, the promise texts rely on a specific, else-where-defined territorial concept. We may assume that at least the priestly texts are implying the same territorial concept of "the land of Canaan" that is clearly defined in the explicit, detailed description found in the Book of Numbers.

THE PROMISED LAND: ANOTHER CONCEPTION

There is, however, one patriarchal narrative which does introduce a more specific statement regarding the territorial extension of the Promised Land. The only territorial statement in the patriarchal promise traditions, it appears at the end of Genesis 15, as part of the covenant with Abraham ("from . . . to" phrases in italic):

> On that day the Lord made a covenant with Abram, saying: "To your offspring I assign this land, *from the river of Egypt to the great river, the river Euphrates*: the Kenites, the Kenizzites, the Kadmonites, the Hittites, the Perizzites, the Rephaim, the Amorites, the Canaanites, the Girgashites, and the Jebusites." (Gen. 15:18–21)

The designation "this land" is followed by a spatial merism ("from the river of Egypt to the great river, the river Euphrates")[30] and an extensive ethnographic list. A comparison to lists of its kind in the Bible shows that this is the most comprehensive one, enumerating a total of ten nations as opposed to the traditional six or seven.[31] It is quite obvious that this language reflects a different territorial conception of the Promised Land than the one carefully delineated in the priestly source (Num. 34). As noted before, this is the foundational text of the concept of Greater Israel, significant even in the current controversy over the borders of the modern state of Israel.[32]

In addition to the promise made to Abraham in Genesis 15, we find similar idioms with respect to the Promised Land in four other locations: the epilogue to the Book of the Covenant, in Deuteronomy, and in the Deuteronomistic literature. A discussion of this concept must therefore take into account all five occurrences of it, and determine their relationship.

First, there is the promise in Genesis 15. Second, the epilogue to the laws of the Book of the Covenant:

> I will set your borders *from the Red Sea to the Sea of Philistia, and from the wilderness to the River*; for I will deliver the inhabitants of the land into your hands, and you will drive them out before you. (Exod. 23:31)

Third, the introduction to the Book of Deuteronomy:

> Start out and make your way to the hill country of the Amorites and to all their neighbors in the Arabah, the hill country, the Shephelah, the Negeb, the seacoast, the land of the Canaanites, and the Lebanon, *as far as the Great River, the river Euphrates*. (Deut. 1:7)

Fourth, in the body of the book:

> Every spot on which your foot treads shall be yours; your territory shall extend *from the wilderness and the Lebanon, and from the River – the Euphrates – to the Western Sea*. (Deut. 11:24)

And fifth, in the Deuteronomic paraphrase of this promise, at the introduction to the Book of Joshua:

> Every spot on which your foot treads I give to you, as I promised Moses. Your territory shall extend *from the wilderness and this Lebanon, to the Great River, the River Euphrates – the whole Hittite country – and to the Great Sea of the setting of the sun* [i.e., the west]. (Josh. 1:3–4)

Scholars have dealt with these texts as though they were "boundary descriptions,"[33] though opinions differ on whether they indicate one territorial unit, or several. This controversy itself implies that as border descriptions, they are not effective or unequivocal. Are they really verbal maps, or do they indicate an altogether different trait of the Promised Land?

Assuming that these are indeed "boundary descriptions," and in accordance with the dominant opinion that all five descriptions indicate one territory (a second possibility will be dealt with later), this land apparently extended from the Euphrates, mentioned in all five sources, encompassing lands on the eastern bank of the Jordan River and the Sinai Peninsula to the Nile. This territorial expanse is inconsistent with the concept of "the land" reflected in patriarchal traditions – as Yehezkel Kaufmann noted, Abraham and Isaac are not at all affiliated with the lands east of the Jordan, and once Jacob crosses that river, he is on foreign soil (Gen. 32:11).[34] It is also at odds with the extent of the land according to the Book of Deuteronomy. This book repeatedly emphasizes that the Promised Land stretched *beyond* the Jordan River, clearly indicating that the lands east of this river are not considered a part of it. For example, Moses declares in his address on the plains of Moab: ". . . that I may cross the Jordan into the land that the Lord our God is giving us" (Deut. 2:29;[35] see also 4:21–22). The verb "cross" (*'br*) is a term designating entry into the land,[36] and the regular formula accompanying the commandments in Deuteronomy states they are to be fulfilled "in the land that you are about to cross into and occupy" (4:14, 22, 26; 6:1; 9:1; 11:8, 11, 31; 30:18; 31:13; 32:47; and also Josh. 1:11).[37] It is very clear that the laws are given for the future, to be observed only after entry into the land, i.e., after crossing the Jordan River: "For you are about to cross the Jordan to enter and possess the land that the Lord your God is assigning to you. When you have occupied it and are settled in it, take care to observe all the laws and rules that I have set before you this day" (Deut. 11:31–32; cf. the heading of the collection of laws that follows in Deut. 12:1). Deuteronomistic historiography also acknowledged the idea that the Jordan is the border of the Promised Land, and its miraculous crossing marked the entry into the land.[38] It is only after the crossing that we hear of the rituals and customs symbolizing the entry: the foundation ritual at Gilgal (Josh. 3–4), the end of the manna (Josh. 5:12), the circumcision of the Israelites

(Josh. 5:2–11), and setting the stones atop Mount Ebal in accordance with the commandment of Deuteronomy 27:2–3 (Josh. 8:30–35). These are the main events narrated in the first part of the Book of Joshua, explaining how possession was taken of the land according to Deuteronomistic historiography.

Furthermore, the biblical concept of the land does not correlate with the assumed broad geographical concept of the Promised Land in other directions as well. In the south, as we have seen, the land supposedly included territory south of Kadesh-barneʻa, as far as the Red Sea. However, the march through the Sinai Desert was outside the Promised Land, according to all sources. The punishment for the sin committed by the spies is to "turn about and march into the wilderness by the way of the Red Sea" (Deut. 1:40), in fulfillment of God's oath: "Not one of these men, this evil generation, shall see the good land that I swore to give to your fathers" (Deut. 1:35). This account does not fit the interpretation of the cited descriptions that the Promised Land extended as far as the Nile.

As for the north, the Deuteronomistic introduction to the Book of Judges notes remaining nations alongside the Israelites inhabiting the territory "from Mount Baal-hermon to Lebo-hamath" (Judg. 3:3), and not as far as the Euphrates.

Moshe Weinfeld has analyzed these texts and their relationship to the territorial unit underlying "the land of Canaan" (Num. 34).[39] He distinguishes between two biblical conceptions of the geographical extent of the Promised Land. The first, referring to "the land of Canaan," was delineated explicitly in Numbers 34:1–12, and was repeated by the prophet Ezekiel in his idealized depiction of the land in the future (Ezek. 47–48). This is the priestly view of the territorial extent of the Promised Land. The second conception, in Weinfeld's opinion, is a broader one, reflecting territory extending between the Euphrates and the Nile, encompassing lands east of the Jordan River as well as the Sinai Peninsula (at least its western coastal strip), and it is expressed by the texts being studied. He suggests that this expansive geographical concept was rooted in a political reality reflecting the military gains of the United Monarchy, an ideal later adopted and embraced by Deuteronomistic ideology. Waldemar Janzen sums up this widely accepted interpretation in the following words: "The second 'map' (Deut 11:24), in this schema, originated in the expansive era of the Davidic-Solomonic empire, was formulated in grand, utopian ancient Near Eastern royal terminology (river to river, sea to sea, etc.), and received its final crystallization by 'the so-called Deuteronomistic author or school' in the Josianic era."[40]

However, it is noteworthy that, unlike "the land of Canaan," the Bible does not assign a name to this specific territory, and scholars refer to it by their own designations, labeling it "imperial borders"[41] or "the border of the patriarchs."[42]

In my view, the assumption that these are "boundary descriptions" is not valid. The Deuteronomistic corpus does not present a set of borders of the Promised Land that differs from the priestly source. The spatial merism expressions we are dealing with are not, in fact, border descriptions, nor purely geographical definitions of the Promised Land. These expressions must be studied as literary-ideological phrases, akin to other merism phrases found in the Bible and in the literature of the ancient Near East.

SPATIAL MERISMS

A few scholars noticed the literary distinctiveness of the "from . . . to . . ." formula characterizing a large portion of so-called border descriptions,[43] but they, too, were unaware of its connection to merism expressions. They were inclined to interpret these territorial terms literally as border descriptions depicting the extremities of the presumed territory, and they tried to detect the two directions or four points of the compass they assumed these descriptions must reflect.

Merism expressions utilize the prepositions "from" and "to" to denote generalizations, presenting a whole (usually abstract) concept, rather than its components.[44] For example, royal building inscriptions from the ancient Near East describe building or reconstructing a structure with the merism: "from its foundation to its parapet";[45] the parallel biblical phrase is: "from foundation to coping" (1 Kings 7:9). These merism expressions are not intended to define the extremities of the structure, but to denote its entire magnitude, its extremities determining the whole and characterizing it.[46] Similarly, spatial merisms express a whole territorial area. They do not refer to a line connecting two places, but designate a whole territorial concept, which the representing sites signify. Thus, for example, the idiom "from Dan to Beer-sheba," found seven times in the

Bible,[47] does not indicate a line linking these two sites, nor does it mean "both Dan and Beer-sheba";[48] rather, it describes the territory and population of "all Israel," as the sweeping statement preceding the idiom in one of the verses states explicitly: "*All Israel*, from Dan to Beer-sheba."[49]

Spatial merisms clearly indicate a territory rather then a line, but what is the significance of the geographical terms joined by the formula "from . . . to . . ."? Studies dealing with merisms treat these terms as border sites, a perception which is grounded in three basic implicit assumptions: that spatial merisms necessarily depict extremities;[50] that the extremities represent directions; and that these directions are opposites – north versus south, east versus west.[51]

However, as will be shown, these assumptions are only partially accurate. Analogous to general merisms, spatial merisms sometimes employ border sites, but at other times the representative sites are located within the territory, or even outside it. General merisms can express totality by extreme members (first and last of a group) when these are set in an ascending or descending order, as for example in the description of the culprits in the story of Sodom: ". . . the townspeople, the men of Sodom, from young to old, all the people to the last man . . ." (Gen. 19:4) – "young" and "old" are the first and last members in the group "the men of Sodom," and so define its sociological borders. However, other merisms may enumerate characteristic members which belong to the same plane and do not correspond to an ascending-descending order. Hezekiah's military victories in Philistine are described by the merism "from watchtower to fortified town" (2 Kings 18:8; cf. 17:9) – "watchtower" and "fortified town" representing the general concept "all places of military importance" without being extremes of any sort. The same is also true for spatial merisms. The representing sites in the above-mentioned idiom "from Dan to Beersheba" do not form a part of the borders of Israel. As noted by Zecharia Kallai, this term "is not to be taken as an indication of the boundaries of Israel's territories. Dan and Beer-sheba are sacred centers in the north and south of the country, respectively, and the borders are, of course, beyond them."[52] Another example is the merism "from India to Nubia" indicating the extent of the vast kingdom of Ahasuerus, "who reigned over a hundred and twenty-seven provinces" (Esther 1:1). India and Nubia are indeed the extreme provinces in the list, India farthest to the east and Nubia to the southwest. However, this merism, too, is not a border description. It provides us with meager information regarding the circumference of the empire, and with no clue at all as to its extent to the north and west. Though this verse is a lovely caption used to accompany maps of the Persian Empire,[53] drawing a map based on this description is practically impossible.[54] Apparently this spatial merism is not meant to represent the geographical borders of the empire, but to give emphasis to the fact that Ahasuerus's rule reached far and exotic lands, that he reigned over the entire civilized world and beyond, India and Nubia serving as prominent representatives of the provinces.[55]

The second implicit assumption common in studies referring to spatial merisms – that the terms placed in them necessarily represent directions – is also only partially correct. In some cases, four sites in a spatial merism can represent the concept of the "four corners of the world," but there is no proof that these sites reflect the directions themselves. Unlike the explicit mention of the directions in the detailed description of the land of Canaan (Num. 34:3, 4, 6, 7, 10), none of the spatial merism expressions address the question of which site depicts which side.

As for the third assumption, a study of biblical texts in which directions are mentioned shows that, besides texts which depict opposite directions (Zech. 8:7; Ps. 75:7),[56] merism expressions might employ directions which are not opposites, as, for example, in the following prophecy of Amos: "Men shall wander from sea to sea and from north to east" (Amos 8:12). "From north to east" disproves that directions must always be opposites. In this unique merism, the prophet juxtaposed a topographic term twice repeated (sea) with explicit directions (north and east). The word "sea" can represent the westerly direction (Gen. 12:8; Exod. 27:12; Josh. 19:34, etc.), and this expression employs four terms, but it obviously does not represent the four points of the compass. Rather than interpreting this phrase as supplementary parallelism and then looking for a complementary southern sea to fill our expectation of the mention of four directions,[57] we should understand the phrase as two parallel merisms. The first merism, "from sea to sea," implying world dominion (Zech. 9:10; Ps. 72:8), prompted another, parallel merism, "from north to east" meaning "in all directions."[58] This phrase illustrates the literary flexibility of merisms. The sites indicating the territory are not necessarily border sites, they do not always represent the four corners, and they are not necessarily opposites. The three common implicit assumptions can no longer be used as a starting point for the discussion of spatial merisms. Rather, each phrase must be determined on its own merits in order to decipher its implied meaning.

SEA AND RIVER, WILDERNESS AND MOUNTAIN

The terms characterizing the spatial merism descriptions referring to the Promised Land are topographical marks – the Euphrates River, the sea, the wilderness, Mount Lebanon. In order to reveal their meaning, we shall first examine their capacity to denote borders.

"The river" is the only one common to all these merisms, recorded in almost uniform language: "to (Deut. 11:24 – "from") the great river, the river Euphrates." One text cites this site as simply "the river" (Exod. 23:31), but no doubt the river with the definite article is the Euphrates (cf. Isa. 8:7).[59] If we follow the usual, literal-geographical rendering of these descriptions, we must seemingly conclude that the Promised Land stretched all the way to the Euphrates – but to which part of it? The general indication "to/from the (great river) river Euphrates" might have meant that this river in its entirety formed the border of the Promised Land, but in the light of other biblical texts this seems impossible, for nowhere does the Bible indicate a land of such vast dimensions. Scholars therefore had to "fill in the blanks" and define, arbitrarily – since none of the texts hint at the possible answer – what part of the river is intended. Usually, the area of the western bend of the river was considered the border of the Promised Land, though some have continued the borderline eastward and northward for quite a distance.[60]

In addition, while attempting to match each site with a given direction, the question arose whether the Euphrates represents the eastern border of the Promised Land, the northern border, or perhaps its northeastern corner.[61] This debate is not merely a petty, pedantic attempt to unify the texts. It bears consequences in regard to the question of the eastern borders of the Promised Land – and, consequently, on the status of the land east of the Jordan. Some scholars are of the opinion that if the Euphrates River is the northern limit of the Promised Land, the lands east of the Jordan River are not considered part of it, whereas when the same Euphrates is used to mark the eastern border, the Promised Land does include the eastern lands. According to John Wijngaards, for example, in the expression "from the river of Egypt to the great river, the river Euphrates" (Gen. 15:18; also 1 Kings 5:1; and 2 Kings 24:7) "only the northern and southern borders are mentioned, and the obvious conclusion is that the eastern border (Jordan) and western (the Sea) are unvarying under any circumstances."[62] In his opinion, Deuteronomy 11:24 intentionally transforms the older concept by shifting the same river from depicting the northern border to the eastern one.[63] In Deuteronomy, Wijngaards explains, the Promised Land does include territories east of the Jordan, in accordance with contemporary political-historical developments in this area. The entire discussion is based on the above-mentioned and refuted assumption that spatial merisms always set opposites: north versus south (river versus wilderness, Exod. 23:31), east versus west (same river versus sea, Deut. 11:24).[64] The uncertainty regarding which direction the Euphrates River represents and the lack of reference to the question of which part of this enormous river actually constituted the border are common to all sources under discussion, and cannot therefore be considered an accidental lapse by the writer(s). The river Euphrates is not a clear marking of any side of the Promised Land, east or north.

"The wilderness," too, appears in most of the sources under discussion (Exod. 23:31; Deut. 11:24; Josh. 1:4). Unlike "the river," which is identified to a high degree of certitude with the Euphrates, the wilderness with the definite article (ha-midbār) is not an accepted label for a specific wilderness.[65] In the area involved, two great deserts are plausible candidates: the Sinai Desert to the south, and the Syro-Arabian Desert to the east. As in the case of the question whether the Euphrates constitutes the eastern or the northern border, here too the identification of the direction that the wilderness represents is considered decisive for the status of the lands east of the Jordan. Scholars arbitrarily identify the wilderness with their "missing side": when lacking a southern border, the wilderness is identified with the Sinai Desert;[66] when an eastern border, it is identified as the great Syro-Arabian Desert.[67] Some scholars who infer that all the expressions refer to the same expanse combine the two and conclude that "the wilderness" refers to both deserts, on the south and the east: "the borderland-desert in the southeast."[68] Again we note that all these conjectures are based not on explicit mention in any of the sources, but on guesses derived from prior assumption. The texts inform us only that the territory shall extend from an unspecified wilderness. Yet, even those who notice the ineffectiveness of a designation like "the wilderness" as a border mark still assume that it fulfills this role in the Promised Land traditions.[69]

A third geographical term appearing in three of the five texts of spatial merisms is the sea, the Mediterranean Sea, also called "the Sea of Philistia" (Exod. 23:31), "the Western Sea" (Deut. 11:24), and "the Great Sea of the setting of the sun (i.e., the west)" (Josh. 1:4). There is no question here as to which side the sea represents, since one of its names indicates this ("the Western Sea"), but here, too, there appears to be a problem regarding the exact location of the borders – where precisely did the northern and southern borders reach this sea? We have no way of deriving this information, crucial for drawing a map, from spatial merisms describing the extent of the Promised Land.

The descriptions mention "the river of Egypt" (Gen. 15:18), which is the Nile,[70] and "the Red Sea" (= *yam sûp*, Exod. 23:31), identified with the Gulf of Aqabah.[71] Like the Euphrates, it is impossible that "the river of Egypt" refers to the Nile in its entirety, and scholars usually constrict the general designation to a part of it, identifying it with the southern border of the Land of Israel.[72] The Red Sea indicates the south,[73] or the east,[74] according to (superficial) scholarly need. In this case, too, the appellation designates a vast body of water, and no clue is given as to what part of it was considered as marking the border. On the basis of the merism expression in Exodus 23:31, the twelfth-century Book of Kuzari by Rabbi Judah Halevi could actually claim that "Sinai and Parān are reckoned as belonging to Palestine, because they are on this side of the Red Sea" (part 2, 14). This is of, course, totally incompatible with the traditions of Israel's wanderings, as mentioned before.

Finally, Mount Lebanon, which appears in the three Deuteronomistic texts (Deut. 1:7; 11:24; Josh. 1:4), presents a double problem. First of all, the term "Mount Lebanon" pertains to an extensive area – a mountain range 170 kilometers (about 105 miles) long and averaging 30 kilometers (about 18 miles) wide – and is therefore very problematic for determining exact borders. Furthermore, one of the descriptions suggests that Mount Lebanon is actually included within the territory of the Promised Land (Deut. 1:7; cf. 3:25), so it is unclear how it can simultaneously define its borders. In consideration of this, some scholars view Mount Lebanon as an intermediary point on a line extending from the south (the wilderness) to the north (the Euphrates),[75] whereas others still maintain that it depicts the northern border of the Promised Land, while its larger part lies within the confines of the land.[76]

Clearly, interpreting the spatial merisms pertaining to the Promised Land as border descriptions creates many problems. The geographical terms they mention are general, related to extensive, vast regions, some of which are unspecified and undetermined (the wilderness, the river). None of the texts correlates the sites with directions; in fact, directions are missing from them altogether. As a result of this typical indistinctness, scholars have an almost free hand in identifying the limits of the Promised Land, some claiming that these descriptions include lands east of the Jordan River, while others claim they do not. The confusion is best illustrated in the attempts to draw a map of the borders of the Promised Land based on these texts. In Weinfeld's map, for example, most lines stay open: the eastern border partially follows the Euphrates from a non-specified point somewhat north of Carchemish; then, somewhere east of the bend in the river, the borderline abruptly turns southward, cutting through the Syro-Arabian Desert to reach the Red Sea at the Gulf of Aqabah. There is no indication of the northern or southern limits of the land.[77]

Problems and questions arise only when the spatial merisms are being forcefully transformed into exact border descriptions, contrary to the impression of indefinite vagueness inherent in them all. If these texts were meant to communicate the exact limits of the Promised Land, or which direction the different terms denote, then they have failed to do so. As we have already seen, the fully detailed description of the land of Canaan (Num. 34:1–12) is able to do just that: to delimit the exact borders of the territory and mark the four directions of the surrounding lines. It seems therefore, that these texts are simply not what scholars have constantly tried to make of them. They are not border descriptions of the Promised Land. The differences between the border description of the land of Canaan (Num. 34:1–12; cf. also Ezek. 47:13–20; Josh. 15–19) and the spatial merisms pertaining to the Promised Land may be summarized as follows:

1. The border description of the land of Canaan contains specific local sites, whereas spatial merisms apply prominent geographical phenomena, with cosmic dimensions (see below).

2. Precise and complete, the border description mentions some twenty place-names, whereas spatial merism expressions mention two to five terms each.

3. The border description conducts a point-by-point virtual tour of the territory's limits, using a system of geographical names connected by verbs. Spatial merisms use the idiom "from . . . to. . . . "

4. The border description presents a complete circumference of the territory. There is no reference to the circumference of the territory the spatial merisms depict.

5. There is an explicit reference to the four directions in the border description. Each is presented by an introductory clause and then described. The spatial merism expressions make no mention of directions.

6. The border description depicts a distinct territory entitled "the land of Canaan" (Num. 34:2). The hypothetical entity underlying the spatial merisms bears no name. As we have seen earlier, the possibility that these references to the Promised Land infer to more than one territorial unit cannot be ruled out.

7. Finally, the two kinds of references to the Promised Land belong to different contexts. The full border description is connected to settlement and inheritance. When delivering his address to Moses, God introduces the description by the title: "this is the land that shall fall to you as your portion, the land of Canaan with its various boundaries" (Num. 34:2). In the ensuing address to the Israelites, Moses instructs them: "This is the land you are to receive by lot as your hereditary portion" (Num. 34:13). The land shall fall to the Israelites as their "portion" or "inheritance," the verb being from the same root *nhl* "receive (their) portion" (Num. 34:13; cf. same root in vv. 17, 18, and 29). The other form of descriptions of the Promised Land, the spatial merisms, are found in the context of war and conquest, tied up with promises of victories over enemies. The first two texts are combined with lists of ethnic groups that God will dispossess for the Israelites (Gen. 15: 19–21; Exod. 23:28). The Deuteronomistic texts explicitly declare the triumphant overcoming of other people preceding and accompanying the occupation of the land: "No man shall stand up to you: the Lord your God will put the dread and fear of you over the whole land in which you set foot, as He promised you" (Deut. 11:25). The differences in form and context reveal that these are two separate genres that convey two different *conceptions* of the Promised Land, but not two dif-

ferent *territorial units*. We shall next explore the meaning of the spatial merisms designating the Promised Land in the light of the geographical terms they apply.

THE PROMISED LAND AND COSMIC BOUNDARIES

The terms figuring in the spatial merisms depicting the Promised Land are large bodies of water, such as seas and rivers, or remote, extreme regions, such as the wilderness or mountainous territories. In ancient Near Eastern traditions these are the areas depicting the very ends of the earth.

In biblical thought the world is comprised of heaven, earth, and sea: "For in six days the Lord made heaven and earth and sea, and all that is in them" (Exod. 20:11; cf. Ps. 135:6). In the ancient worldview the sea encompassing the earth was deemed external to habitation, a chaotic element outside the realm of world order, and therefore an opponent to orderly forces and an imminent danger. Consequently, the sea plays a major role in *chaoskampf* myths in ancient Near Eastern mythologies, most prominently the well-known battle of Marduk with Tiamat, the sea monster in the Babylonian epic Enuma elish, and the divine struggle of Baal with "Prince Yam, judge River" in Ugaritic myth.[78] Biblical literature reflects a profound acquaintanceship with *chaoskampf* myths, and, while processing these traditions in a characteristic manner – polemicizing with, adapting, or altogether rejecting them – in their new form one can still identify traces of motifs of the divine battle with insurgent water familiar from the ancient Near Eastern myths (i.e., Isa. 27:1; Ps. 74:13–15; Job 26:12–13).[79] The Red Sea mentioned in Exodus 23:31 plays a special role in Israelite rendering of the *chaoskampf* myths, in the story of its crossing at the time of the exodus (Exod. 13–15).[80] According to several biblical hints, the struggle ended when God incarcerated Sea, putting it under watch (Job 7:12), banning its invasion of the realm of order. God is the one "who set the sand as the boundary to the sea, as a limit for all time not to be transgressed" (Jer. 5:22; cf. Ps. 104:9; Prov. 8:27–29). Thus, the sea is external to land, which serves as a boundary for it, and vice versa: the sea, according to ancient Near Eastern worldview, surrounds the earth, delimiting the land and confining it.[81] This mythological role of the sea encircling the earth is perhaps connected to its conception, even in modern times, as the "ultimate border," as Lord Curzon, who coined the term "natural border," stated: "Of all natural Frontiers the sea is the most uncompromising, the least alterable, and the most effective."[82]

Besides the sea, rivers are also prominent in spatial merisms describing the Promised Land. River and sea are poetic parallels in Ugaritic literature – as the designation of Baal's opponent "Prince Yam, judge River" indicates – as well as in the Bible: "For He founded it (the earth) upon the ocean, set it on the rivers" (Ps. 24:2). Rivers are but extensions of the mythological ocean surrounding earth and are therefore also bodies of water delimiting earth, reverberating with cosmic and mythological connotations: "Are You wroth, oh Lord, with Rivers? Is your anger against Rivers, Your rage against Sea . . . ?" (Hab. 3:8). Both the Euphrates and the Nile are called "sea" in biblical sources, evidence of the conception that these huge rivers were indeed seen as extensions of cosmic water (for the Euphrates, see Jer. 51:36; for the Nile, see Ezek. 32:2. Cf. also Pharaoh's image as dragon [tanin] lying in the sea [Isa. 27:1; Ezek. 32:2]).[83]

The appearance of broad bodies of water in spatial merisms pertaining to the Promised Land – sea and river, and especially the Great Sea (in its alternate names) in three of the descriptions, and the Euphrates mentioned in all of them – indicates a strong affinity of these descriptions to universal borders. Since promise terminology leans on ancient Near Eastern cosmology, local wadis, which are dry riverbeds (Job 6:15), do not figure in these texts. A prominent landmark, "Brook (or wadi) of Egypt" is mentioned seven times in the Bible in the context of boundary descriptions.[84] We find it besides Euphrates in the spatial merism, "from the Brook of Egypt to the river Euphrates" (2 Kings 24:7; its reverse in Isa. 27:12) reflecting the territory of Syria-Palestine after the conquests of Nebuchadnezzar from Egypt in the years 605–604 B.C.E.[85] But it has no place in descriptions of the Promised Land.[86]

Even a river like the Jordan, boasting a regular, albeit fluctuating in quantity, flow of water, is conceived as no more than a local river, running from the Sea of Galilee to the Dead Sea. It is not deemed a "universal river" like the Euphrates or the Nile and therefore is never actually entitled "river" (nahar) in the Bible, as mentioned above. The Jordan definitely plays a central role in descriptions of the borders of Israel in such texts as the detailed delineation of the Land of Canaan (Num. 34:12), and we even find it in a merism designating the conquered land in the

Deuteronomistic summary and review of the conquest of the land: "See, I have allotted to you, by your tribes, these nations that still remain, and that of all the nations that I have destroyed, *from the Jordan to the Mediterranean Sea* of the setting of the sun (i.e., the west)" (Josh. 23:4).[87] This historiographic text coined a unique hybrid merism in order to bridge the gap between Promised Land terminology, relating to universal extent, and the known borders of the land extending to the Jordan.[88] In a like manner the merisms characterizing the Promised Land do not mention the Sea of Galilee or the Dead Sea, local bodies of water not belonging to the category of cosmic oceans.

In addition to cosmic water, three of the descriptions mention the wilderness, without specification (Exod. 23:31; Deut. 11:24; Josh. 1:4). The wilderness, too, was deemed external to habitation, a place of hiding and refuge for peripheral social elements, nomads, and lawless persons, as reflected in such biblical stories as Hagar's flight from Sarah (Gen. 16:6–14), David's escape from King Saul (1 Sam. 22:2; 23–26), or Elijah's hiding in the desert in fear of Jezebel (1 Kings 19:3–4)[89] and outside the Bible in the story of the escape of King Idrimi to the desert (ca. 1500 B.C.E.).[90] The wilderness is a place haunted by demons (Isa. 13:21; 34:11–14),[91] the dwelling place of harming destructive winds, a "terrible land" (Isa. 21:1) depicted in terms similar to those describing the underworld.[92] In the Bible the same is said about the ends of the earth (Jer. 25:32–33), and it is most probable that these two concepts overlap – wilderness located at the ends of the earth.[93] As Shemaryahu Talmon has pointed out, these attributes are the source for the motif of the wilderness as a place of passage in the Bible, representing on the historical and eschatological level the passage from chaos to order/cosmos.[94] In biblical depictions of God the almighty, creator and ruler of earth, God is specifically able to control chaotic elements, such as water and wilderness: "He turns the rivers into a wilderness, springs of water into thirsty land, fruitful land into a salt marsh. . . . He turns the wilderness into pools, parched land into springs of water" (Ps. 107:33–35).

The Lebanon mountain range also reflects the view that lofty mountains depict the extremities of earth.[95] In Mesopotamia mountains served as a place of hiding and refuge[96] and were considered a dwelling place of chaotic elements, such as the mythic lion-faced eagle Anzu, who stole the Tablet of Destinies from the chief god Enlil and fled with it to the mountains, threatening world order.[97] Mountains were created side by side with the watery deep and the sea (Isa. 40:12 and elsewhere), and in language reminiscent of *chaoskampf* phraseology, God's theophany proves the rebellious nature of the mountains mentioned next to that of the sea: "He rebukes the sea and dries it up, and He makes all rivers fail; Bashan and Carmel languish, and the blossoms of Lebanon wither. The mountains quake because of Him, and the hills melt" (Nah. 1:4–5a).[98]

In Assyrian royal inscriptions the "evil enemy" is depicted as putting his trust in natural elements, such as wide seas and inaccessible mountains, for his protection – precisely the places in which he is forced to find refuge after his consequent defeat.[99] In light of the role of seas and rivers and wilderness and mountains in the ancient Near Eastern worldview as denoting the ends of the world, it becomes clear why these are precisely the elements appearing in spatial merisms characterizing the Promised Land. These are representatives of the most prominent geographical elements, signifying the world in general and its boundaries in particular.

ASSYRIAN IMPERIAL DESCRIPTIONS

The concept, as well as the literary form, of the spatial merisms depicting the Promised Land are known from Neo-Assyrian imperial propaganda. Royal inscriptions mention general formulations claiming control over the entire earth, without reference to specific sites or places, continuing an ancient Mesopotamian tradition. Already in the Middle Assyrian period, cosmic rule involved claims of control over the remotest parts of the earth: surrounding seas, overwhelming deserts, and inaccessible mountains, related to mythological cosmogonic traditions. Thus, Tukulti-ninurta I (1243–1207) is crowned as "king of the upper seas and the lower seas, king of the mountains and the wide deserts."[100]

In the Neo-Assyrian period, claims to world rule contained detailed descriptions of the actual military exploits of the kings. Aššurnaṣirpal II (883–859) proclaimed:

> (I am the) conqueror from the opposite bank of the river Tigris to Mount Lebanon and the Great Sea of the land Amurru in the west, the entire land of Ḫatti, (I who) have gained dominion from the source of the River Subnat to the extensive land Urumu, the entire

lands Nairi; I conquered the entire land Laqû; I subdued the land Suḫu to the land Rapiqu; I regarded as people of my land (inhabitants) from the pass of Mount Kirruru to the land Gilzānu, from the pass of the city Babitu to the land Namru; I brought within the boundaries of my land from the opposite bank of the lower Zab to the city Tīl-Bāri which is upstream from the land Zaban, to the city Tīl-ša-Zabdāni and the city Tīl-ša-Abtāni, the cities Ḫirimu (and) Ḫarutu, fortresses of Karduniaš.[101]

Spatial merisms in this king's summary are not all of one kind. He starts with cosmic elements (Mount Lebanon, the Great Sea) hinting at world dominion, and then moves on to more detailed and specific sites (passes in mountains, cities mentioned by name) in order to substantiate and demonstrate his claim. In this part of the king's statement we do find local rather than cosmic elements, illustrating his victories and conquests. The summary appears in many versions and seems to have been updated in accordance with the king's real achievements: Mount Lebanon and the Great Sea, for example, are mentioned only in later versions, after the king reached them.

His successors, Šalmaneser III and Adad-nīrārī III, made similar statements about their campaigns. Šalmaneser III (859–824) claimed:

I subdued (the territories) from the source of the Tigris to the source of the Euphrates, from the sea of the interior of the land Zamua to the sea of Chaldaea.[102]

And Adad-nīrārī III (811–783) stated:

I subdued from the bank of the Euphrates, the land Hatti, the land of Amurru in its entirety, the land of Tyre, the land of Sidon, the land of Humri (Samaria), the land of Edom, the land of Palastu, as far as the Great Sea in the west.[103]

Tiglath-pileser III (745–727) defined the horizons of his empire in a foundation stele:

Palace of Tiglath-pileser, [the great king, the mighty king, king of Assyria, king of Babylon, king of Su]mer and Akkad, king of the four quarters, the brave warrior who with the help of Ashur, his Lord, [smashed like pots all the unsubmissive,] swept over them like the [flo]od, made them as powerless ghosts; the king who [marched about] at the command of Ashur, Shamash and Marduk, the great gods, [*from*] *the bitter sea of Bit-Yakin up to Mount Bikni in the east, and up to the Western Sea as far as Egypt,* [*from*] *the horizon to the zenith,* he ruled and reigned over the countries.[104] (emphasis added)

These are detailed reports of military achievements stating specific places and people. However, they are not border descriptions. The kings recount the major lands and cities conquered in alien territory, emphasizing heroic deeds. They mention mountains and seas, rivers and faraway lands, in accordance with the notion of world rule. The message is an ideological claim of universal rule cast in the form of reports of actual achievements. Tiglath-pileser III further celebrated his rule over the countries by the formula "[from] the horizon to the zenith," adding a cosmic dimension to the commemoration of his enterprise.[105]

Other inscriptions of Neo-Assyrian rulers conform to this concept. Their actual military conquests were represented in similar style, depicting a continuous movement of territorial expansion to the horizons and beyond. This remained one of the most prominent themes in royal inscriptions, an important aspect of Neo-Assyrian self-justification and ideological motivation till the fall of the empire.

Stylistically, it is important to note that these statements are expressions of totalities, replete with spatial merisms, accompanied by lists of places, countries, and people which came under the Assyrian yoke.[106]

The prominent geographical elements typifying the formulas in promise terminology are found here as well: seas, mountains, rivers, and deserts. The great Neo-Assyrian conquerors set specific geographical names to prove their claim for world dominion (i.e., Mount Bikni, the Tigris River, the Euphrates, the Western Sea). These expressions bear typological and actual resemblance to the promise in Deuteronomy (11:24), a resemblance which is increased in the paraphrastic quotation in the Deuteronomistic introduction to the book of Joshua: "Your territory shall extend *from the wilderness and the Lebanon, to the Great River, the River Euphrates – the whole Hittite country – and to the Great Sea of the setting of the sun* [i.e., the west]." (Josh. 1:4). The description reads like an Assyrian royal declaration, and there is a perfect match between the place names: Lebanon, the whole Hittite country (missing from Deuteronomy),[107] and the Great Sea (Western Sea in Deuteronomy).[108] Lists of conquered peoples and lands in the royal inscriptions are reminiscent of the list of nations found in Genesis 15 – "To your offspring I assign this land, from the river of Egypt to the great river, the river Euphrates: the Kenites, the Kenizzites, the Kadmonites, the Hittites, the Perizzites, the Rephaim, the Amorites, the Canaanites, the Girgashites, and the Jebusites" (Gen. 15:18–21) – and the list of places in the introduction to Deuteronomy – "Start out and make your way to the hill country of the Amorites and to all their neighbors in the Arabah, the hill country, the Shephelah, the Negeb, the seacoast, the land of the Canaanites, and the Lebanon, as far as the Great River, the river Euphrates" (Deut. 1:7).

The difference lies not in the details of form and content or in the message, but in the background of the descriptions. Royal Neo-Assyrian propaganda refers to past events. Actual achievements of the king are utilized to illuminate his claim of fulfilling the role of a great king, expanding the frontiers of his rule, appropriating new areas and subordinating their dwellers to the Assyrian yoke. Biblical promise traditions are just that: a promise to be fulfilled in the future, that is, Israel's vocation. But they both speak of military success followed by maximal rule over territories and people. This is clear from the subsequent verse in Deuteronomy, "No man shall stand up to you: the Lord your God will put the dread and the fear of you over the whole earth (*kōl ha-'areṣ*) in which you set foot, as He promised you" (Deut. 11:25), and from the explanation following the spatial merism in the epilogue to the laws of the Book of the Covenant: "I will set your borders from the Red Sea to the Sea of Philistia, and from the wilderness to the River; *for I will deliver the inhabitants of the land (ha-'areṣ) into your hands, and you will drive them out before you*" (Exod. 23:31).

Biblical phraseology thus reflects the image of the self-convinced political-religious persuasion which "oiled the wheels" of the Assyrian war machine. Assyrian sources indicate that this was a value system which asserted a qualitative difference between center and periphery – order and chaos, good and evil, Assyrian and foreigner – ultimately justifying Assyrian imperial rule as a natural, religious right. It was an official system aimed at, in the words of Mario Liverani, "justification of imbalance and exploitation."[109] Biblical authors were exposed to Assyrian imperial propaganda, whether through written or visual sources, or oral communication.[110] In converting Assyrian territorial imperial images to the notion of promised Israelite political greatness, biblical authors, in particular of the Deuteronomistic school, were responding to the ideological pressure inaugurated by the Assyrian maelstrom. According to them, the political greatness which Assyrian kings boast of was already promised to the people of Israel in the formative period.

CONCLUSION

The promise reflected in spatial merisms is not to be understood literally, nor should it be translated and transformed into border lines on maps. It is a promise of world dominion, as in fact the Deuteronomistic text states explicitly: "*Every spot on which your foot treads shall be yours*; your territory shall extend from the wilderness to the Lebanon and from the River – the River Euphrates – to the Western Sea" (Deut. 11:24, quoted in Josh. 1:3–4). Analogous to our understanding of the phrase "every spot on which your foot treads" as a literary idiom, highlighting the totality of the military success and territorial expansion promised to the people of Israel, rather than literally, as a promise to grant her the actual territories tread upon by the people,[111] we should interpret the juxtaposed spatial merism as a literary idiom and not literally as a border description. The spatial merisms referring to the Promised Land do not present a second concept of the extent of the land, contrary to the one comprehensively delineated in the priestly source (Num. 34). Their difference from that concept has nothing to do with geography, such as whether or not the territories east of the Jordan are included in or excluded from the Promised Land. In the Bible there is only one map of the borders of the Promised Land, and it refers to an entitled, specific political entity: "the land of Canaan." The five spatial merisms describing the Promised Land present an altogether different *concept* of it, and not just a different *extent*. Theirs is not an image of a delimited piece of land, bordering on neighboring states, each with its own territory. The spatial merisms in promise terminology reflect a land that has no borders at all, only ever-expanding frontiers; they are referring to universal rule, using stock terminology typical of Neo-Assyrian royal inscriptions.

NOTES

1. For rivers as natural borders, see Nili Wazana, "Water Division in Border Agreements," *State Archives of Assyria Bulletin* 10 (1996): 55–66.

2. For the list of rivers, see Philippe Reymond, *L'eau, sa vie, et sa signification dans l'ancien testament*, Supplements to Vetus Testamentum, vol. 6 (Leiden: E. J. Brill, 1958), 86–87; Luis I. J. Stadelmann, *The Hebrew Conception of the World*, Analecta Biblica, vol. 39 (Rome: Biblical Institute Press, 1970), 161–62.

3. See the typical description: "On three sides Palestine is surrounded by natural borders: to the West the Mediterranean, 'the Great Sea' of the Bible; on the east and south the desert"; Yohanan Aharoni, *The Land of the Bible: A Historical Geography*, 2d ed., rev. and enl., trans. from Hebrew by Anson F. Rainey (Philadelphia: Westminster Press, 1979), 64. While geographically correct, political entities seldom encompassed all the area as far as the eastern desert.

4. For these two distinctive characteristics of the land, see ibid., 3–42.

5. Translations of biblical passages are based on the Jewish Publication Society's *Tanakh: A New Translation of the Holy Scriptures according to the Traditional Hebrew Text* (Philadelphia: Jewish Publication Society, 1985) (hereafter cited as JPS), but in some cases have been altered toward a more literal translation.

6. On the relationship of the first eleven chapters of Genesis to the main Pentateuchal theme and the Land as the primary motif in the Bible, see Harry M. Orlinsky, "The Biblical Concept of the Land of Israel: Cornerstone of the Covenant between God and Israel," in *The Land of Israel: Jewish Perspectives*, ed. L. A. Hoffman (Notre Dame, Ind.: University of Notre Dame Press, 1986), 27–64. See also Moshe Weinfeld, "The Inheritance of the Land," in his *The Promise of the Land* (Berkeley and Los Angeles: University of California Press, 1993), 183–84.

7. The JPS translation is inconsistent in rendering the verb *ntn*, sometimes as "assign" (Gen. 12:7, 17:8, 24:7, 28:4, 13, 35:12, 48:4), sometimes as "give" (13:15, 17), and as "grant" when referring to the blessing (28:4).

8. Albrecht Alt was the first to distinguish between two separate components of the divine promise: posterity and the possession of the land. However, he ascribed them to different social and historical backgrounds, one originating before the entry into Canaan – "the concern of a nomadic tribe for the maintenance and the increase of its numbers" – and the other, formed in Palestine, being "the claim of settlers to their own land"; see "The God of the Fathers," in Albrecht Alt, *Essays on Old Testament History and Religion* (Oxford: Basil Blackwell, 1966), 65. (The original German article was published in 1929.) An interest in great numbers is, of course, not exclusive to nomadic societies and is closely related to times of national pride. Ronald Clements identifies three elements in the patriarchal promises: possession of land, growth into a great nation, and becoming a

blessing to the nations of the earth; Ronald E. Clements, *Abraham and David: Genesis XV and Its Meaning for Israelite Tradition*, Studies in Biblical Theology, vol. 5 (London: SCM Press, 1967), 57.

9. Jon D. Levenson, *The Death and Resurrection of the Beloved Son* (New Haven and London: Yale University Press, 1993), 97. See also Gen. 17:20–21.

10. Moshe Weinfeld, "The Covenant of Grant in Old Testament and Ancient Near East," *Journal of the American Oriental Society* (hereafter cited as *JAOS*) 90 (1970): 184–203; 92 (1972): 468–69; idem, *Deuteronomy and the Deuteronomic School* (Oxford: Oxford University Press, 1972), 74; idem, "The Covenantal Aspect of the Promise of the Land to Israel," in Weinfeld, *The Promise of the Land*, 222–64.

11. As the prominent element of the covenant, it is interesting to note that the promise of the land appears only in the blessings to Abraham and Jacob. The only land promise text that concerns Isaac applies a unique plural form, twice repeated: "Reside in this land and I will be with you and bless you; I will assign *all these lands* to you and to your offspring, fulfilling the oath that I swore to your father Abraham. I will make your descendants as numerous as the stars of heaven, and give to your descendants *all these lands*, so that all the nations of the earth shall bless themselves by your offspring – in as much as Abraham obeyed me . . ." (Gen. 26:3–5). The clear distinction between "this land," where Isaac is told to remain, and "all these lands," which will be granted to his descendants in return, illustrates that the author is not referring to the concept of the Promised Land as a geographical entity. A comparison with God's oath to Abraham in the second angelic address to him after the binding of Isaac (22:15–18), where the root *šb'*, oath/to swear, also appears, shows that the phrase "and give to your descendants all these lands" is parallel to "and your descendants shall seize the gates of their foes" (22:17), reaffirming that it is not a promise of the land, but a blessing of dominion and military superiority. (For the reverberations of the stories of Abraham in this oracle to Isaac, see Levenson, *Death and Resurrection*, 141, though he understands this to be a reiteration of the Abrahamic promise with all its components: progeny, blessing, and land.) However, the priestly account (P) of the promise to Jacob mentions a former grant of the land to Isaac as well: "The land that I assigned to Abraham and Isaac, I assign to you" (35:12). The deficiency of an explicit land promise in the accounts of Isaac must be attributed therefore to the place he holds between the narratives of his more dominant father and son.

12. On this see Peter Machinist, "Outsiders or Insiders: The Biblical View of Emergent Israel and Its Contexts," in *The Other in Jewish Thought and History*, ed. Laurence J. Silberstein and Robert L. Cohn (New York: New York University Press, 1994), 35–60.

13. Since Second Temple times, the divine imperative to Abraham to leave his

homeland and set out for an unknown destination was seen as the first of a series of ten trials (for example, The Book of Jubilees 17:17; Mishna Avot 5:3 – cf. Maimonides' commentary).

14. This is reflected in one of the Aramaic translations of this phrase: "Up, walk the land and establish your legal claim to it" (Targum Pseudo-Jonathan to Gen. 13:17). The practice of land survey before receiving title to it is reflected in Josh. 18:4; 24:3; see also the saying of R. Eliezer in Bava Bathra 100:a; cf. Arnold B. Ehrlich, *Randglossen zur Hebräischen Bibel* (Leipzig: J. C. Hinrichs, 1908), 1:53.

15. The JPS renders the word *ha-'areṣ* as "ground," and indeed it can mean ground as well as earth and land; cf. L. Koehler and W. Baumgartner, *The Hebrew and Aramaic Lexicon of the Old Testament*, rev. ed. (Leiden: E. J. Brill, 1994), s.v. However, given the context of the promise, the translation "*the land* on which you are lying" is preferable here. After all, the promise does not allude to the specific clods of earth on which Jacob lay, but to the land in its entirety.

16. David Daube, *Studies in Biblical Law* (Cambridge: Cambridge University Press, 1947), 26–39. Daube rightly distinguishes between literary texts using land transfer motifs and terminology and actual legal documents, such as the acquisition of land in Jer. 32:6ff.

17. See Claus Westermann, "Promise to the Patriarchs," in *Interpreter's Dictionary of the Bible*, supp. vol. 1976, 692a; Orlinsky, "Biblical Concept" (n. 6 above), 31–32.

18. Jacob J. Rabinowitz, "The Susa Tablets," *Vetus Testamentum* 11 (1961): 61–63; Weinfeld, "Covenant of Grant" (n. 10 above), 199–200.

19. On this interpretation of the passage, see Daube, *Biblical Law*, 28.

20. For the priestly mark of these designations, see John Skinner, *A Critical and Exegetical Commentary of Genesis*, 2d ed., The International Critical Commentary (Edinburgh: T. and T. Clark, 1930), 289.

21. Out of eleven texts alluding to the promise of the land, only one possibly contains an indication to its limits, the covenant with Abraham (Gen. 15:18–21, which will be dealt with below). The promise is mentioned in the following ten texts (designations of the land emphasized): "Raise your eyes and look out from where you are, to the north and south, to the east and west, for I give *all the land that you see* to you and your offspring forever" (13:14–15); "Up, walk about *the land*, through its length and its breadth, for I give it to you" (13:17); "I am the Lord who brought you out from Ur of the Chaldeans to assign *this land* to you as a possession" (15:7); "I assign *the land you sojourn in* to you and your offspring to come, *all the land of Canaan*, as an everlasting holding" (17:8); "I will assign *this land* to your offspring" (24:7); "May He grant the blessing of Abraham to you and your offspring, that you may possess *the land where you are sojourning*, which God assigned to Abraham" (28:4); "*The land* [JPS: *the ground*] *on which you are lying* I will

assign to you and your offspring" (28:13); "*The land that I assigned to Abraham and Isaac, I assign to you; and to your offspring to come will I assign the land*" (35:12); "And I will assign *this land* to your offspring to come for an everlasting possession" (48:4).

22. Cf. the following citation from Peter Machinist, "Palestine," *The Anchor Bible Dictionary* (New York: Doubleday, 1992), 5:69 (hereafter cited as *ABD*): "'Palestine' here will be understood essentially as the territories comprising the biblical Israel and Judah."

23. For the priestly origins of Numbers 34, see Samuel R. Driver, *An Introduction to the Literature of the Old Testament* (1897; reprint, Gloucester, Mass.: Peter Smith, 1972), 69.

24. For a map drawn on the basis of this description and it's parallel in Ezekiel 47–48, see Aharoni, *Land of the Bible* (n. 3 above), 70.

25. This mention appears in the treaty between Hattusili III and Benteshina of Amurru. See Ernst F. Weidner, *Politische Dokumente aus Kleinasien*, Boghazköi Studien, Heft 8–9 (Leipzig: J. C. Hinrichs, 1923), 124:6; and Gary Beckman, *Hittite Diplomatic Texts*, 2d ed., Writings from the Ancient World, SBL, vol. 7 (Atlanta: Scholars Press, 1999), 101, § 2. For the relationship of Amurru and Hatti, see Itamar Singer, "A Concise History of Ammuru," in *Amurru Akkadian: A Linguistic Study*, ed. Sh. Izre'el, Harvard Semitic Studies, vol. 41 (Atlanta: Scholars Press, 1991), 2:135–238. According to this account, Aziru, king of Amurru, received a document defining the borders of his land; however, all surviving copies of the treaty between Aziru and Suppiluliuma – three in Akkadian and one in Hittite – lack a border description (for the Akkadian copies, see Weidner, *Politische Dokumente aus Kleinasien*, 76–79; for the Hittite version, see Johannes Friedrich, *Staatsverträge des Hatti-Reiches in hethitischer Sprache*, vol. 2, Mitteilungen der Vorderasiatisch-Ägyptischen Gesellschaft, Bd. 31/2 (Leipzig: J. C. Hinrichs, 1926), 1–48; translations by Albrecht Goetze, *Ancient Near Eastern Texts Relating to the Old Testament*, ed. James B. Pritchard, 2d ed. (Princeton: Princeton University Press, 1969), 529–30 (hereafter cited as *ANET*); Beckman, *Hittite Diplomatic Texts*, 36–41. It may be that the border description appeared in a part of the document missing from all extant versions, or perhaps was issued to Aziru in a separate document similar to the edicts issued to the king of Ugarit; Beckman, *Hittite Diplomatic Texts*, 173–77, no. 31.

26. Murshili II warns the local rulers of the lands of Arzawa in western Anatolia not to violate their neighbors' territory, thus upsetting the carefully balanced new order he imposed upon them. See, for example, the following admonition in the treaty with Manapa-Tarḫunta of the land of the Šeḫa River: "Look, I, My majesty, [have given] you [Manap]a-Tarḫunta the land of the Šeḫa River and the land of Appawiya. This shall be your land, protect it! [I have gi]ven Mašuilu[wa]

the land of Mira and the land of Kuwali[ya]. And I have given Targasna[li] the land of Ḥappala. This shall be your land, protect it!" Johannes Friedrich, *Staatsverträge des Hatti-Reiches in hethitischer Sprache*, vol. 2, Mitteilungen der Vorderasiatisch-Ägyptischen Gesellschaft, Bd. 34/1, (Leipzig: J. C. Hinrichs, 1930), 12–15, § 10, ll. 15–19; Beckman, *Hittite Diplomatic Texts*, 84, § 7.

27. I.e., the description of borders closing the Akkadian treaty between Tudḥaliya II of Hatti and Shunashshura of Kizzuwatna, at the beginning of the fourteenth century B.C.E.; Beckman, *Hittite Diplomatic Texts*, 24–25, §§ 60–64.

28. I.e., the borders between Ugarit and Mukish, its northeastern neighbor, and Siyanu-Ushnatu, its southern neighbor; ibid., 173–78.

29. I.e., the border of the land of Hatti and the land of Mira-Kuwaliya outlined in the treaty between Murshili II and Kupanta-Kurunta, one of the Arzawan kings; ibid., 76, § 9.

30. The term "spatial merism" will be dealt with below.

31. The list of ten nations is a collection of "everything that was known of ancient names"; Gerhard von Rad, *Genesis*, 3d ed., The Old Testament Library (hereafter cited as OTL) (London: SCM Press, 1972), 189. For the lists, see Tomoo Ishida, "The Structure and Historical Implications of the Lists of Pre-Israelite Nations," *Biblica* 60 (1979): 461–90.

32. For an example of the role of this text in contemporary debate, see the following portrayal of Israeli "fundamentalists, who cling to creating Greater Israel, as outlined in Abraham's covenant with God"; Robin Wright, *Time Magazine*, 22 May 2000, 109.

33. Cf. Aharoni, *Land of the Bible* (n. 3 above), 67.

34. Yehezkel Kaufmann, *The Religion of Israel* (in Hebrew) (Tel Aviv: Bialik Institute and the Dvir Co., 1947), 2:304.

35. Weinfeld demonstrated that the historiographical framework of the Book of Deuteronomy portrays the possession of the lands east of the Jordan River in language reminiscent of the possession of the promised land (Deut. 1–3), and applies on it the rules of the ban (*ḥerem*, Deut. 2:34–35; 3:6–7; cf. Deut. 20:15). He therefore suggested that the Deuteronomic ideology considered the lands east of the Jordan as part of the Promised Land. See Moshe Weinfeld, "The Extent of the Promised Land: the Status of Transjordan," in *Das Land Israel in biblischer Zeit*, ed. Georg Strecker, Göttinger Theologische Arbeiten, Bd. 25 (Göttingen: Vandenhoeck & Ruprecht, 1983), 67–68; idem, "The Borders of the Promised Land: Two Views," in idem, *The Promise of the Land* (n. 6 above), 69–75. Deuteronomy 2:25 is explained by Weinfeld as an unconscious reflection of the older conception of the Promised Land as stretching westward beyond the river; Moshe Weinfeld, *Deuteronomy 1–11*, The Anchor Bible (New York: Doubleday, 1991), 172. See, however, note 37 below.

36. See Peter Diepold, *Israels Land*, Beiträge zur Wissenschaft vom Alten und Neuen Testament, 5/15 (Stuttgart: W. Kohlhammer, 1972), 29.

37. This is a typical Deuteronomic phrase, as demonstrated by Weinfeld's list in *Deuteronomy and the Deuteronomic School* (n. 10 above), 342. The fact that it also appears in the Deuteronomic sources (Josh. 1:11) illustrates the centrality of the idea that the Jordan River formed the eastern border of the land in Deuteronomic circles, rendering Weinfeld's dismissal of it as an unconscious lapse unlikely.

38. Diepold, *Israels Land*, 29.

39. Moshe Weinfeld, "Extent of the Promised Land (n. 35 above), 59–75; idem, *The Promise of the Land* (n. 6 above), 52–75; See Waldemar Janzen, "Land," *ABD*, 4:146.

40. Janzen, "Land."

41. Weinfeld, "Extent of the Promised Land," 69; idem, *The Promise of the Land*, 69.

42. On "the patriarchal border," see Zecharia Kallai, *Biblical Historiography and Historical Geography: Collection of Studies* (Frankfurt am Main: Peter Lang, 1998), 116. See also the label "the 'Patriarchs' borders'," in Nadav Na'aman, *Borders and Districts in Biblical Historiography*, Jerusalem Biblical Studies, vol. 4 (Jerusalem: Simor, 1986), 244–45.

43. Magne Saebø, "Grenzbeschreibung und Landideal im Alten Testament mit besonderer Berücksichtigung der min-ʿad-Formel," *Zeitschrift des Deutschen Palästina-vereins* 90 (1974): 14–37; Aharoni, *Land of the Bible* (n. 3 above), 86–87. See also Nadav Na'aman's distinction: "These borders do not belong to the same category as the other two, for they are defined only by the 'from . . . to . . .' formula," *Borders and Districts*, 245.

44. Scholars seldom fail to quote Honeyman's definition: "Merismus, which is a figure of speech akin in some respects to synecdoche, consists in detailing the individual members, or some of them – usually the first and last, or the more prominent – of a series, and thereby indicating either the genus of which those members are species or the abstract quality which characterizes the genus and which the species have in common"; Alexander M. Honeyman, "Merismus in Biblical Hebrew," *Journal of Biblical Literature* 71 (1952): 13–14. Cf. Hendrik A. Brongers, "Merismus, Synekdoche und Hendiadys in der Bibel-Hebräischen Sprache," *Oudtestamentische Studiën* 14 (1965): 1; Joze Krašovec, *Der Merismus*, Biblica Orientalia, vol. 33 (Rome: Biblical Institute Press, 1977), 3; Wilfred G. E. Watson, *Classical Hebrew Poetry*, JSOT Supplement Ser., vol. 26 (Sheffield: JSOT Press, 1984), 322. Watson concludes that "Merismus, then, is an abbreviated way of expressing a totality" (321). The term "merism" originated in the Greek "merismus," meaning a part of the whole; see Krašovec, *Der Merismus*, 1.

45. See Wolfram von Soden, *Akkadisches Handworterbuch* (Wiesbaden, 1965), 1422, s.v. *uššu* I 3; *The Chicago Assyrian Dictionary* (hereafter cited as *CAD*) vol. G., p. 1, s.v. *gabadibbû*; vol Š I, p. 486, s.v. *šaptu* 3a.

46. Krašovec's definition is useful here: "Der Merismus druckt also eine Ganzheit, eine Totalität aus. Dadurch wird die symbolische Gegebenheit des Merismus evident: Die einzelnen Termini besitzen nicht eine realistische Bedeutung, sondern stehen symbolisch-stellvertretend für die gesamt Realität oder Gattung einer gegebene Ebene"; Krašovec, *Der Merismus*, 3.

47. Judg. 20:1; 1 Sam. 3:20; 2 Sam. 3:10; 17:11; 24:2, 15; 1 Kings 5:5. With reversed order, this expression is found in 1 Chron. 21:2; 2 Chron. 30:5. This reversal of word order is a case of "diachronic chiasm" as demonstrated by Avi Hurvitz, "'Diachronic Chiasm' in Biblical Hebrew," in *Bible and Jewish History: Studies in Bible and Jewish History Dedicated to the Memory of Jacob Liver*, ed. B. Uffenheimer (in Hebrew) (Tel Aviv: Tel Aviv University, 1972), 248–55, Eng. summary on pp. xxv–xxvi.

48. Cf. Honeyman, "Merismus in Biblical Literature" (n. 44 above), 11–12.

49. "All Israel" here corresponds to the modern term "nation": a group of people settled in a specific territory sharing a history and a founding ancestor; Steven Grosby, "Religion and Nationality in Antiquity," *Archive Européennes de Sociologie* 32 (1991): 229–65.

50. Honeyman was of the opinion that spatial (as well as temporal) merisms always denote extremes and that this semantic practice was the source of merisms in general: "It is instructive to trace the origin of the idiom. *Min . . . we-'ad . . .* is used, quite naturally and regularly, to express the limits of time or place within which something exists or happens"; Honeyman, "Merismus in Biblical Literature," 11.

51. For a study utilizing all three underlining assumptions, see Saebø, "Grenzbeschreibung und Landideal" (n. 43 above).

52. Zecharia Kallai, *Historical Geography of the Bible* (Jerusalem: Magnes Press; Leiden: E. J. Brill, 1986), 309.

53. E.g., the map of the Persian Empire in Luc H. Gollenberg, *Atlas of the Bible* (London and Edinburgh: Nelson, 1956), 95, map 21.

54. Compare to the map mentioned in the previous note and historical maps of the Persian empire; for example, *Historical Atlas of Iran* (Tehran: Danishgah, 1971), plate 5.

55. See Sandra B. Berg, *The Book of Esther: Motifs, Themes, and Structure*, Society of Biblical Literature Dissertation series, vol. 44 (Missoula, Mont.: Scholars Press, 1979), 33.

56. In this psalm, the wilderness apparently represents the south and mountains the north; Shemaryahu Talmon, "Midbār," *Theological Dictionary of the Old*

Testament (hereafter cited as *TDOT*) (Grand Rapids, Mich.: Scholars Press, 1997), 8:98. This is not, in fact, a merism expression, but it does employ specific directions as opposites.

57. Medieval commentaries identified two real seas in the term "from sea to sea": the Red Sea to the south and the Mediterranean to the west (Ibn-Ezra, David Kimhi, *Metzudat David*, in *Miqra'oth Gedoloth* [The Rabbinic Bible], Commentaries of Rashi, Abraham ibn Ezra, David Kimchi, and Meṣudoth [New York: Pardes, 1961]). Cf. the emendation suggested by the JPS translation of the phrase "from south to west." Modern commentators understood it as referring to the wandering from the eastern end of the country to the west, that is, from the Dead Sea to the Mediterranean (or vice versa). For this and other suggestions along these lines, see Shalom M. Paul, *Amos*, Hermenia (Minneapolis: Fortress, 1991), 266.

58. Choice of north and east – nonparallel sides – may indicate a special interest in or emphasis on these sides. Paul suggested that Amos, the prophet from the southern kingdom of Judah, does not mention the south since it denoted the place of the temple; therefore, wandering in vain, seeking "the word of the Lord," may be a deliberate hint at where the answer lay (Paul, *Amos*). Cf. also Isa. 49:12; Ps. 107:3.

59. See Reymond, *L'eau* (n. 2 above), 87–88. The only river with the definite article in the Bible indicating another river is mentioned in a description of one of the Edomite kings, "Shaul of Rehoboth-on-the-river" (Gen. 36:37), designating a local river in northern Edom; see Skinner, *Genesis* (n. 20 above), 436. This exception to the rule is explicated by the nature of the special source in which it is found, probably an Edomite document; see John R. Bartlett, "The Edomite King-List of Genesis XXXVI. 31–39 and I Chron. I. 43–50," *Journal of Theological Studies* 16 (1965): 301–14. In Mesopotamian documents, too, an unspecified "river" is always the Euphrates; *CAD* vol. N I, 373, s.v. *nāru* 3'k. The Egyptian ruler Thut-mose III (1490–1436) describes the Euphrates as "that great river which lies between this foreign country and Naharin." See *ANET*, 240.

60. See map 2 in Weinfeld's *The Promise of the Land* (n. 6 above), 57, in which he traces the border according to Genesis 15:18–21 along the bend of the Euphrates, stopping somewhere north of Carchemish. Compare Diepold's statement that there is no telling exactly where one must draw the border line connecting the Euphrates with the Mediterranean; Diepold, *Israels Land* (n. 36 above), 32.

61. Jan A. Soggin, *Joshua*, OTL (London: SCM Press, 1972), 29. Along the same lines, Talmon states that the Euphrates designates east when opposed to the sea (Deut. 11:24) and north when contrasted with the wilderness (Ex. 23:31), since *midbār* in his opinion "serves in the OT to demarcate the southern boundary of the 'Promised Land.'" See his "Midbār" (n. 56 above), 98.

62. John N. M. Wijngaards, *The Dramatization of Salvific History in the Deutero-nomic Schools*, Oudtestamentische Studiën (Leiden: E. J. Brill, 1969), 95. The Red Sea was seen as designating the eastern border, instead of the Jordan, so the description in the epilogue to the laws of the Book of the Covenant (Exod. 23:31) did not depict the borders of "Greater Israel" but indicated a narrower image; see Wijngaards, *Dramatization of Salvific History*, 94, n. 1; Magne Saebø, "Vom Grossreich zum Weltreich," *Vetus Testamentum* 28 (1978): 88–89.

63. Wijngaards, *Dramatization of Salvific History*, 98.

64. The same underlying assumption governs Saebø's discussion of these passages. See Saebø, "Grenzbeschreibung und Landideal" (n. 43 above), 17.

65. Contra Talmon, who proposed that *ha-midbār* must be the Sinai Desert, see Shemaryahu Talmon, "The 'Desert Motif' in the Bible and in Qumran Literature," in *Biblical Motifs: Origins and Transformations*, ed. Alexander Altmann, Studies and Texts, vol. 3 (Cambridge, Mass.: Harvard University Press, 1966), 42.

66. Diepold, *Israels Land* (n. 36 above), 33; Volkmar Fritz, *Das Buch Josua*, Handbuch zum Alten Testament, Reihe 1, Bd. 7 (Tübingen: Mohr, 1994), 28. Saebø believes that the eastern border is the Jordan throughout all descriptions, and so the wilderness constantly symbolizes the south; Saebø, "Grenzbeschreibung und Landideal," 18.

67. Weinfeld identifies the terms mentioned in Exod. 23:31 with directions as follows: "The Sea of Reeds constitutes the southern end of the land (Aqaba). The 'sea of the Philistines' represents the western boundary; the 'wilderness' represents the eastern border, and 'the River' (Euphrates) the northern border." Moshe Weinfeld, "Zion and Jerusalem as Religious and Political Capital: Ideology and Utopia," in *The Poet and the Historian*, ed. Richard E. Friedman, Harvard Semitic Studies (Chico, Calif.: Scholars Press, 1983), 98. However, the same verse is interpreted by him somewhat differently elsewhere: "The Sea of Reeds is at the southernmost point of the land (the Gulf of Aqabah); the Sea of Philistia (the Mediterranean) constitutes the western and southwestern border; 'the wilderness' is the eastern and southern border; while 'the River', the Euphrates, is the northern and northeastern border." Weinfeld, *The Promise of the Land* (n. 6 above), 67.

68. Kallai, *Biblical Historiography* (n. 42 above), 117; cf. Weinfeld, *The Promise of the Land*, 67; Soggin, *Joshua* (n. 61 above), 29.

69. See, for example: ". . . wilderness areas are less suited for demarcation of political boundaries than are seas, rivers, and mountain ranges. Despite this, midbār (and also ʿarābâ) serves in the OT to demarcate the southern boundary of the 'Promised Land'"; Talmon, "Midbār" (n. 56 above), 98.

70. I.e., Skinner, *Genesis* (n. 20 above), 283. According to a different opinion, "the River of Egypt" mentioned here is identical to "the Brook (or wadi) of Egypt"

found in a few biblical spatial merisms, such as "from Lebo-hamath to the Wadi of Egypt" (1 Kings 8:65; for other occurences of this term, see n. 84 below); see Claus Westermann, *Genesis: A Commentary*, vol. 2, *12–36*, trans. J. J. Scullion (Minneapolis: Augsburg Pub. House, 1985), 229. Others claim the text in Genesis 15 should be emended from "river" (*nahar*) to "brook" (*naḥal*); see the comment of the Biblia Hebraica Stuttgartensia (hereafter cited as BHS) to this phrase. Cf. Ephraim A. Speiser, *Genesis*, The Anchor Bible (New York: Doubleday, 1964), 114; Clements, *Abraham and David* (n. 8 above), 21, n. 24.

71. John R. Huddlestun, "Red Sea," *ABD*, 5:633–34.

72. In Hermann Gunkel's words, the Nile as Israel's border is "a grand hyperbole"; Hermann Gunkel, *Genesis* (Macon, Ga.: Mercer University Press, 1997), 182 (trans. from 3d ed., 1910).

73. See quotations from Weinfeld in n. 67 above.

74. Wijngaards, *The Dramatization of Salvific History* (n. 62 above), 94, n. 1. According to his interpretation, the description in the epilogue to the laws of the Book of the Covenant (Exod. 23:31) did not depict the borders of "Greater Israel" but indicated a narrower image (see also Saebø, "Vom Grossreich zum Weltreich" [n. 62 above], 88–89).

75. See Diepold, *Israels Land* (n. 36 above), 33; Saebø,"Grenzbeschreibung und Landideal," 19. Soggin, too, remarks: "The Lebanon, rather than being a fixed landmark, is a point of great importance, included in the territories of Israel"; Soggin, *Joshua* (n. 61 above), 30. The mediaeval commentator Rashbam (R. Samuel ben Meir) already tried to identify the landmarks with directions, consequently ignoring Lebanon altogether: "From the Wilderness: south. The Euphrates River: north. To the western Sea: from the place where you are standing now, the southeastern corner of the Land of Israel to the Mediterranean in the west" (his commentary to Deut. 11:24).

76. For example, Shmuel Aḥituv, *Joshua: Introduction and Commentary* (in Hebrew), Mikra Leyisra'el (Tel Aviv: Am Oved, 1995), 73.

77. Weinfeld, *The Promise of the Land* (n. 6 above), 57.

78. For an English translation of Enuma elish, see Benjamin R. Foster, *Before the Muses* (Bethesda, Md.: CDL Press, 1993), 351–402. For the Ugaritic texts, see Mark S. Smith, *The Ugaritic Baal Cycle*, vol. 1, Supplements to Vetus Testamentum, vol. 55 (Leiden: E. J. Brill, 1994), 235–36. In Egypt the subjugation of a water monster is enumerated among divine deeds benefiting humanity in the instructions of Meri-ka-re; see Miriam Lichtenheim, *The Context of Scripture*, vol. 1, ed. W. W. Hallo (Leiden: E. J. Brill, 1997), 65, col. 2 and n. 29 there; Otto Kaiser, *Die mythische Bedeutung des Meeres in Ägypten, Ugarit und Israel*, Beihefte zur Zeitschrift für die Alttestamentliche Wissenschaft, 78 (Berlin: A. Toepelmann, 1962), 36. See also the Hittite myth "Iluyanka," where the storm god battles a

snake adversary at sea, in *Hittite Myths*, trans. Harry A. Hoffner, Jr., 2d ed., SBL Writings from the Ancient World Series, vol. 2 (Atlanta: Scholars Press, 1998), 13, § 25.

79. Of the numerous studies dealing with this subject, I will mention a few: Hermann Gunkel, *Schöpfung und Chaos in Urzeit und Endzeit* (Göttingen: Vandenhoeck & Ruprecht, 1895), who coined the term *chaoskampf*; Arent J. Wensinck, *The Ocean in the Literature of the Western Semites*, Verhandelingen de koninklijke akademie van Wetenschappen te Amsterdam, Deel 19, no. 2 (Amsterdam, 1918); Mary K. Wakeman, *God's Battle with the Monster* (Leiden: E. J. Brill, 1973); and John Day, *God's Conflict with the Dragon and the Sea*, University of Cambridge Oriental Publications no. 35 (Cambridge: Cambridge University Press, 1985). See also Umberto Cassuto's attempt to trace what he supposed must have been an ancient Israelite epic on the subject of the rebellion of sea against the creator: Umberto Cassuto, *Biblical and Oriental Studies*, trans. from Hebrew and Italian by Israel Abrahams (Jerusalem: Magnes Press, 1973), 2:69–109.

80. This is probably "historicized" myth: see Samuel E. Loewenstamm, *The Evolution of the Exodus Tradition*, trans. from Hebrew by Baruch J. Schwartz (Jerusalem: Magnes Press, 1992), 233–92; Bernard F. Batto, "The Reed Sea: Requiescat in Pace," *Journal of Biblical Literature* 102 (1983): 27–35. Some have even suggested deriving the Hebrew name of this sea (*sûp*) from *yam sôp*, "end or border sea," finding support in the LXX translation of this term in 1 Kings 9:26; see discussion in Huddlestun, "Red Sea" (n. 71 above), 637b–38a.

81. See Wensinck, *The Ocean*, 21–22; Reymond, *L'eau* (n. 2 above), 170. For the Egyptian conception of the ocean encircling the earth, see Mario Liverani, *Prestige and Interest: International Relations in the Near East ca. 1600–1100 B.C.*, History of the Ancient Near East, Studies, vol. 1 (Padova: Sargon, 1990), 52–53.

82. Quoted by Albert K. Weinberg, *Manifest Destiny* (Chicago: Quadrangle Books, 1935), 64.

83. Stadelmann's note (n. 2 above), 56, that this designation stems from natural conditions – the widening of the Euphrates and the Nile at the end of their course (at the Persian Gulf and the Delta, respectively) – is simplistic and overlooks the heavy mythological charge these texts convey. An Egyptian text similarly parallels Euphrates and the sea (see Liverani, *Prestige and Interest*, 60, n. 3), and this river was considered a substitute or representative of the ocean (there, p. 53).

84. Designating the southern border of Judah (Josh. 15:4, 47), which is identical to the southern border of the "Land of Canaan" (Num. 34:5; 1 Kings 8:65 = 2 Chron. 7:8; in the shortened form "the Brook," Ezek. 47:19; 48:28), and as an element in the spatial merism: "from the Brook of Egypt to the river Euphrates" (2 Kings 24:7, its reverse Isa. 27:12). For our discussion it is immaterial whether

we identify the Brook of Egypt with Wadi el-'Arish, as already done in Hellenistic sources, or with Nahal Besor, as suggested by Nadav Na'aman, "The Brook of Egypt and Assyrian Policy on the Border of Egypt," *Tel Aviv* 6 (1979): 68–90, and criticized by Anson F. Rainey, "Toponymic Problems (cont.): The Brook of Egypt," *Tel Aviv* 9 (1982): 131–32.

85. See Mordechai Cogan and Hayim Tadmor, *II Kings*, The Anchor Bible (New York: Doubleday, 1988), 307–8. This phrase is certainly connected to conceptions of universal rule, but it is also based on a historical territorial unit.

86. Liverani, *Prestige and Interest* (n. 81 above), who noticed the connection of land descriptions in the Bible and cosmological conceptions, failed to differentiate between descriptions of the Promised Land and historiographical depictions and wondered how it was possible that the Brook of Egypt, which is a dry wadi most of the year, was upgraded to represent cosmic ocean forming the southern border of the land (ibid., p. 54). See also identifications of "Brook of Egypt" with "River of Egypt" mentioned in n. 70 above.

87. The Deuteronomic nature of this chapter is evident both from typical phraseology and its form as a farewell address from a prominent leader to the people; see Martin Noth, *The Deuteronomistic History*, Journal for the Study of the Old Testament Supplement Series, 15 (Sheffield: JSOT Press, 1981), 9, 102, n. 15; Weinfeld, "The Covenant of Grant" (n. 10 above), 10–14.

88. The same merism appears also in the Septuagint version to Josh. 13:7–8a, again in a Deuteronomic summary. After the words "for the nine tribes and the half-tribe of Manasseh" (verse 7b), the Greek adds: "from the Jordan to the Mediterranean Sea in the west you shall assign it, the Great Sea will border it. For the two tribes and the half tribe of Manasseh." This version relieves the current difficulty of a literary unit dealing with the two and a half eastern tribes commencing with "The Reubenites and the Gadites along with it . . ." (8a), and was probably lost due to homoeoteleuton "and the half tribe of Manasseh." See Lea Mazor, "The Septuagint Translation of the Book of Joshua" (in Hebrew) (Ph.D. diss., The Hebrew University of Jerusalem, 1994), 265; cf. Samuel Holmes, *Joshua: The Hebrew and Greek Texts* (Cambridge: Cambridge University Press, 1914), 56. Thus, in the Greek version, this hybrid merism frames the unit dealing with the tribal allotments.

89. Talmon, "The 'Desert Motif'" (n. 65 above), 42. For the various meanings of biblical *midbār*, see Armin W. Schwarzenbach, *Die geographische Terminologie im Hebräischen des Alten Testamentes* (Leiden: E. J. Brill, 1954), 93–98.

90. For an English translation of Idrimi's tale, see Leo Oppenheim, *ANET*, 557–58. For wilderness as home of nomads, see also *CAD* Ṣ, 145, s.v. ṣēru, 3f.

91. Cf. *CAD* Ṣ, 145–46, s.v. ṣēru, 3g.

92. The Sumerian word for wilderness (EDIN) and its Akkadian counterpart

(ṣēru) also depict the underworld; see Alfred O. Haldar, *The Notion of the Desert in Sumero-Accadian and West-Semitic Religions*, Uppsala Universitet Årsskrift, 3 (Uppsala: A. B. Lundequistska Bokhandeln, 1950), 19–20, 35. In the lament for Ur, the destructive element is described as a storm rising from the desert; see Thorkild Jacobsen, *The Harps that Once . . .: Sumerian Poetry in Translation* (New Haven and London: Yale University Press, 1987), 455, l. 111; and Haldar, *Notion of the Desert*, 28.

93. In the Bible the ends of the world are not portrayed explicitly, dubbed "the ends of the earth," "*apsey 'ereṣ*," a term echoing Akkadian Apsû (see further below), the cosmic underground water (Mic. 5:3; Ps. 72:8 etc.), or "*qᵉtzotey 'ereṣ*" (Isa. 40:28; Ps. 48:11, etc.); and "the remotest parts of the earth," "*yarkᵉtey 'ereṣ*" (Jer. 6:22). See also Stadelmann, *Hebrew Conception of the World* (n. 2 above), 135.

94. Talmon, "The 'Desert Motif'" (n. 65 above), 37. The ritual of driving a goat out into the desert for 'Azazel (Lev. 16:7–10, 22) also reflects the roles of the desert (ibid., 44).

95. Mountains filled a double role, as the edges of earth and as its center or navel; see Shemaryahu Talmon, "Har," *TDOT*, vol. 3 (Grand Rapids Mich.: Scholars Press, 1978), 431.

96. See *CAD* Š1, 55, s.v. *šadû* 1j.

97. For the Anzu epic, see Amar Annus, *Epic of Anzu*, State Archives of Assyria Cuneiform Texts, vol. 3 (Helsinki: Vammalan Kirjapaino Oy, 2001).

98. Compare this to the actions of the god Erra, who is depicted as ruler of the universe and said to "convulse the sea, obliterate mountains," The Epos of Erra, IIId l. 5; English translation in Foster, *Before the Muses* (n. 78 above), 778, l. 5. Nahum here is clearly drawing from "a general stock of so-called mythological storm imagery, which is well known elsewhere in the Bible and the Canaanite world beyond"; Peter Machinist, "The Fall of Assyria in Comparative Ancient Perspective," *Assyria 1995*, ed. Simo Parpola and Robert M. Whiting (Helsinki: Helsinki University Press, 1997), 182.

99. Frederick M. Falles, "The Enemy in Assyrian Royal Inscriptions: 'The Moral Judgement'," *Mesopotamien und Seine Nachbarn*, 25th Rencontre Assyriologique Internationale, ed. Hans J. Nissen and Johannes Renger (Berlin: Dietrich Reimer Verlag, 1982), 428.

100. Albert K. Grayson, *Assyrian Rulers of the Third and Second Millennia* B.C., The Royal Inscriptions of Mesopotamia, Assyrian Records (hereafter cited as RIMA), 1 (Toronto: University of Toronto Press, 1987), 244, ll. 5–7.

101. Albert K. Grayson, *Assyrian Rulers of the Early First Millennium* B.C., vol. 1, RIMA 2 (Toronto: University of Toronto Press, 1991), 309, ll. 19b–27.

102. Albert K. Grayson, *Assyrian Rulers of the Early First Millennium* B.C., vol. 2, RIMA 3 (Toronto: University of Toronto Press, 1996), 95, ll. 18–19a.

103. RIMA 3, 213, 11–13.

104. Text and translation in Hayim Tadmor, *The Inscriptions of Tiglath-Pileser III King of Assyria* (Jerusalem: The Israel Academy of Sciences and Humanities, 1994), 159, ll. 1–4.

105. Hayim Tadmor, "World Dominion: The Expanding Horizon of the Assyrian Empire," in *Landscapes: Territories, Frontiers, and Horizons in the Ancient Near East*, History of the Ancient Near East, Monographs, 3, no. 1, ed. L. Milano et al. (Padova: Sargon, 1999), 57.

106. See Liverani, *Prestige and Interest* (n. 81 above), 46–47.

107. The Septuagint version, where these words are absent, does not prove their secondary nature in the Massoretic text (contra BHS), but points to an attempt to increase the similarity with the text in Deuteronomy. Similarly, "the Great Sea" was altered to "the western Sea" in Greek; Mazor, "The Septuagint Translation" (n. 88 above), 134–35.

108. As noted by Weinfeld, "Zion and Jerusalem" (n. 67 above), 97–98.

109. Mario Liverani, "The Ideology of the Assyrian Empire," in *Power and Propaganda*, ed. Mogens. T. Larsen, Mesopotamia, vol. 7 (Copenhagen: Akademisk Vorlag, 1979), 297–317.

110. For the use of Neo-Assyrian images in biblical literature, see Peter Machinist, "Assyria and Its Image in the First Isaiah," *JAOS* 103 (1983): 719–37.

111. The phrase in the blessing, "Every spot on which your foot treads shall be yours" (Deut. 11:24; Josh. 1:3), is used to stress the opposite, too. When passing by the territories of the neighboring nations, Edom, Moav, and Ammon, God warns: "Do not provoke them. For I will not give you of their land so much as a foot can tread on; I have given the hill country of Seir as a possession to Esau" (Deut. 2: 5; cf. verses 9, 19). The blessing seems to be a reversal of a curse formula of reducing a country's size to a place that a person could not stand on, a place the size of a brick, that is found in Assyrian treaty phraseology: "May (his) territory, (reduced) to the size of a brick of 1 cubit, be annihilated for his sons . . . to stand upon" (treaty of Ashur-nirari V [754–745] and Mati-'ilu king of Arpad, I 5'–7'. See Simo Parpola and Kazuko Watanabe, *Neo-Assyrian Treaties and Loyalty Oaths*, SAA, vol. 2 (Helsinki: Helsinki University Press, 1988), 8. Carlo Zaccagnini offers a similar reading for a curse passage in the Pazarcik stele; see Carlo Zaccagnini, "Notes on the Pazarcik Stela," *State Archives of Assyria Bulletin* 7 (1993): 55, n. 7.

A SENSE OF PLACE:
THE MEANING OF HOMELAND IN
SACRED YORÙBÁ COSMOLOGY

JACOB K. OLÚPÒNÀ

For some strange reason, perhaps traceable to colonialism and Western missionary campaigns, the study of religion and the comparative history of religions that developed in America and Europe did not have any significant impact on the study of religion in Africa. Africa lacks a comparative history of religions like that pioneered by Mircea Eliade, Charles Long, and other scholars of the Chicago school.

Heavily influenced by Christian theological perspectives, many African scholars sidestepped the "comparative history of religions" and adopted a spurious approach to African indigenous religions, as though looking through Judeo-Christian spectacles or as if clothing indigenous religious experiences in foreign garments. Pioneered by Geoffrey Parrinder, Bólájí Ìdòwú, John Mbiti, and others, contemporary religious scholars continue to sidestep the comparative history approach, thus incurring the anger of many other scholars outside the African religious circle, including British anthropologist and philosopher Robin Horton and Kenyan agnostic Okot Pitek. Indeed, Robin Horton, in an earlier publication, labeled these founding fathers "members of the devout opposition." One of the concerns of Horton and Pitek was that scholars of African religions should abandon models that they thought continue to pose irrelevant questions to African religious traditions. A discourse on African religions that asks whether Africans are monotheistic or polytheistic entirely misses the point. Rather, conceptual and analytical issues should be examined that are implicit within a tradition.

Paradoxically, at the time this debate was going on, some scholars of human geography were analyzing African cultural traditions and religions through structuralism, spatialized schemes, and metaphor. However, because cross-disciplinary study was unfashionable then, scholars of African religions paid little, if any, attention to studies in what we now know as cultural geography and the geography of religion, developed using the same ethnographic data to arrive at more creative, African-centered interpretations. The pioneering works of G. J. Afọlábí Òjó and Paul Wheatley on the Yorùbá of western Nigeria were the first to analyze the significance of spatial dimensions in Yorùbá religious traditions and culture.

In this paper, I shall use general observations of Wheatley, Òjó, and Mircea Eliade as a template for examining the significance of place and space in Yorùbá religious experience and imagination. My aim is to begin to correlate the history of religions scholarship linked to place with spacial metaphors in the study of African religions. First, let us examine how scholars of comparative history and religions theorize about sacred place cross-culturally.

SACRED PLACE IN COMPARATIVE HISTORY OF RELIGIONS: THEORETICAL CONSIDERATIONS

Few have given more significance to place and space in the understanding and interpretation of religion than Mircea Eliade. His works, though heavily criticized by members of his own academic clan, can pass as durable classics in the history of religions. Eliade attempted to develop a structural theory, among many others, in which religion is experienced primarily in spatial terms. He observed that human cultures create special places essentially symbolizing centers of the universe. These sacred places are designed for humans to communicate with the ultimate being. These sacred places function as a cosmic novel, "through which the divine enters the material world and from which that world is oriented."[1]

Likewise, Eliade's theory holds that the center is important to human religious experience and the habitable world.[2] As Eliade observes: "If the world is to be lived in, it must be founded – and no world can come to birth in the chaos of the homogeneity and relativity of profane space. The discovery or projection of a fixed point – the center – is equivalent to the creation of the world."[3] While Eliade's concept of spatial metaphor as normative theory with universal application has been called into question, Jonathan Z. Smith criticized Eliade for "overemphasizing the significance of centers,"[4] and anthropologist Roy Rappaport observed that Eliade "seriously overvalued the case for the priority of space in the religious experience."[5]

Undoubtedly, the works of Mircea Eliade and Emile Durkheim on the sacred have largely influenced the perceptions and understandings of place among historians of religion. For Eliade, the sacred is that set apart from the profane, or the secular. However, when such delineation is applied to specific cultures and societies – such as the Yorùbá or Native Americans – strictly speaking, an oppositional definition may be inconsistent with these traditions. Jane Hubert, scholar of aboriginal societies, for example, informs us that although "the literal translation of *waahi tapu* is 'sacred place,' . . . the modern translation of tapu as 'sacred' fails to capture its true essence, for the deep spiritual value of waahi tapu transcends mere sacredness."[6] Moreover, Jonathan Smith underscores the importance of two forms of religious orientation: locative and utopian (placeless) religions. In the Yorùbá imagination, home is, as Smith aptly observes, a home place, a center where one locates one's self and being. It is at the same time a place of memory and nostalgia for the past. It conveys deep meanings for individuals and the collective.[7] Diasporic religion, on the other hand, exhibits no place or placelessness in the existing world. Nevertheless, often corroborated by scholars within and outside the field of religion, Eliade's spatial metaphors provide a basis with which to begin interpreting African religious experiences.

In *God's Place in the World: Sacred Space and Sacred Place in Judaism*, Seth Kunin suggests two models of sacred space: the dynamic and the static.[8] Dynamic sacred space, like the moving camp, remains untied to any particular location. In Jerusalem's Temple of Solomon, static sacred space is fixed in a unique location. In dynamic sacred space, sacred space is tied directly to sacred peoples.[9] As Kunin notes, "Dynamic sacred place is temporary and disassociated from physical space"; it is "fluid," for "Any place can become contextually sacred."[10] The reference to the sacred here, as often used in the history and phenomenology of religion, implies the recognition that something (an object, site, or person) is "placed apart from everyday things or places, so that its special significance can be recognized and rules regarding it obeyed."[11] Place occupies a significant category in the phenomenology of African religion because place is regarded as the site where individuals, origins, and ends are located. It has metaphorical and ontological significance to individuals and to the collectivity of people. In the context of Yorùbá religion, sacred place and sacred space normally correspond to the static centralized model, where place is "associated with a historical and mythological experience of the divine."[12]

In recent years, Mircea Eliade's theory has been reinvigorated, especially among scholars of the Chicago school who are applying the method and theory of the history of religions and their interpretive orientations of land, space, and territory. Davíd Carrasco, Charles Long, Lawrence Sullivan, Mary MacDonald, and Philip Arnold, to mention only a few, are engaged in new interpretations of place and space. These scholars have revived the study of what we may call, for lack of better terminology, the "spatiality of matter" or the "materiality of religion."

I would like to apply these new interpretations to the sacredness of place in Yorùbá religious traditions, examining both their universality and specificity in the many cultural regions comprising the Yorùbá of southwestern Nigeria. I will also question the significance of concepts developed in the history of religions discipline. For the Yorùbá people, place defines a people's origin and end. It implies a metaphysical and ontological impact on individuals and the collectivity. The sacredness of place is often defined in relationship to an opposition. Those who are outsiders to the place are considered in their imagination incapable of recognizing the territory's sacred qualities, its significance to its mythic history, and the very *being* of its inhabitants.

The Yorùbá philosophical concept of place may best be understood by the ancestral proverb *Ọmọ onílẹ̀ tẹẹ jẹ́jẹ́, àjòjì tẹẹ wùrùwùrù* ("While the owners of a place tread very gently on it, the stranger treads very roughly"). A "foreigner" or "outsider" remains incapable of recognizing the numerous signs and symbols that mark the sacredness of the insider's territory. While outsiders may recognize physical mannerisms and the significance of a place other than their own, they may be unwilling to accept the sacredness of such place because it stands beyond the location of their own sacred place and space.

This proverb also carries a metaphorical meaning. *Tẹẹ jẹ́jẹ́* refers to an ancestral masquerade's drumbeat, signifying a "slow dance," for example, illustrated by the ancestral Egúngún festival in Òkè-Igbó, a Yorùbá town in Ondo State and my mother's home place. As another example of differentiation between insiders and outsiders, the New Yam festival celebrates the auspicious, autochthonous spirit and owner of the lands and territory of Ilẹ̀-Olúji, a nearby town in Ondó State and my wife's hometown in Nigeria. At the height of the festival, the natives are led by their king (Jẹgun) toward a place of high ritual. Loudly shouting *"oogbèrì kúrò"* ("outsiders leave"), the insiders drive away all non-indigenes to prevent outsiders from viewing a deity's Ọlọ́fin earthly propitiation.

There are yet deeper levels invoked by sacred place in the Yorùbá imagination. Sacred place carries none of the signifiers often portrayed in the history of religion. It is not restricted or "confined" to easily recognizable sites, but may encompass a larger space, often unmarked in Yorùbá cities. I have noticed that in a procession – either a carnival, parade, or any ceremony commemorating funeral rites or rites of passage – suddenly the drummers may stop drumming at a certain place. The cessation of the drum may signify the burial place of a cultural hero, a mythic personality, or the site of certain sacred events occurring in the beginning of time.

When viewed in their historical contest, the land and space considered sacred remain part of the identity and spiritual self-definition of the people who claim the place. This claim is especially relevant when a group or an individual is defined in relationship to a place, space, or territory.

THE PHENOMENON OF PLACE: YORÙBÁ RELIGIOUS EXPERIENCE

There is no better starting point for raising contextual issues on the significance of place for Yorùbá religious experience than Paul Wheatley's scholarship. Wheatley believed that civilization is based on the growth of the city-state. In his archetypal work, *The Pivot of the Four Quarters*, Wheatley develops an analysis of the cross-cultural significance of urbanism. He identifies seven primary regions of world civilizations, including the Yorùbá of southwestern Nigeria. He categorizes these civilizations into a typology that serves as a framework of analysis. For Wheatley, ritual and religious ceremonies help to define complex systems of defense, commercial relations, and emerging market economies. In any society, as ceremonial centers grew in importance, these centers became public ceremonial structures, symbolic of cosmic, social, and moral order. Similarly, these centers operated as institutions that controlled developing political economies. These structures regulated the distribution of resources and served as a means for creating different hierarchies of elites within the society.

The phenomenology of Yorùbá religious experience and expression should recognize Yorùbá sacred geography. Central to sacred geography is the experience of place and space identities. Topographical features and important geographic landmarks are endowed with religious meanings as events embody the cosmology and worldview. They provide meaning and distinction to the Yorùbá people and places. We can argue that the entire fabric of the Yorùbá religious system resembles a record of places, activities, and peoples in experiences of religious significance.

Yorùbá construction of place emanates from a perception of space, imagination, mythology, and history. Such perception may differ from what we call the secular perception of place. Dorothea Theodoratus and Frank LaPena note about the sacred geography of the northern California Wintu: "the qualities of a place or a region which make them sacred, as well as the concomitant reverence and spiritual activities of the native practitioners, are profoundly different from mainstream perceptions of these places, attitudes and actions."[13]

I will begin my analysis and description of Yorùbá experience of place with the Yorùbá myth of creation, rather than with an inventory of Yorùbá sacred geography. I will touch on the primary expression of the Yorùbá world – the people, the place, ritual sacrifice, institutions of sacred kingship, as well as the propagation of gods, ancestors, and spirits that have their origin in the experience of place.

YORÙBÁ COSMOLOGY AND THE NATURAL WORLD

The power of the natural world is prominently featured in creation myths of Yorùbá society and in the Yorùbá conception of the universe in general. In the most cited Yorùbá myth of origin, Olódùmarè, the Supreme Being, decided to create the world. He gave Ọbàtálà, one of the gods, a mythical five-toed chicken, along with a quantity of earth in a small shell and a chain, with instructions to descend into the universe and perform the ritual of creation. On his way to carry out Olódùmarè's assignment, Ọbàtálà met other divinities who were drinking. He joined them, got drunk, and fell asleep. Another divinity, perhaps a female named Odùduwà, overheard Olódùmarè's message and saw Ọbàtálà fast asleep. Odùduwà picked up the materials for performing the tasks to create the world. She descended from the sky into the world with the aid of the chain. Reaching the earth, she poured out the soil from the shell onto the primal water and placed the mythical fowl upon it. The chicken scattered the earth around, creating dry land on the water. Afọlábí Òjó, a cultural geographer, graphically describes the extraordinary primordial phenomenon that the earth-spreader performed:

> The mighty bird, a special giant bird, descended on the sand and used its huge claws to dig, and spread out the sand. Where the claws dug deep, valleys were formed. Hills, uplands, and mountains were left within the interstices of the claws.[14]

The place where Odùduwà accomplished this task was named Ilé-Ifẹ̀ (the place where the earth spreads). The "earth-spreader" symbol motif represented by the chicken is a significant African religious and art motif.

The Yorùbá creation story, like most cosmogonies, presents many themes and motifs quite familiar to the historian of religions. It begins with the recognition of primordial water out of which the universe emerged. It recalls a theogony, the epiphany of the Òrìṣà and divine human beings into the created world. Through creation, the worlds of the divinities and of humans merged, and a horizontal relationship, a passage up and down, was established between gods and humans, creative forces, and creation itself. The universe thus created was not an empty one. Through the activities of the divine being, Odùduwà, the basic elements of the universe and the earth's morphology became established. Dry and wet lands, vegetation, animal and plant life were firmly entrenched. The palm nut, which Odùduwà planted, became the tree of life that gave birth to the world of vegetation. It is also an important element in the Ifá divination process with which people discern the wishes of heaven.

The creation myth also suggests that at the time of creation, Olódù-

Fig. 1. Shrine of Ọbàtálá in Ilé-Ifẹ̀ (Photo: Jacob Olúpọ̀nà)

Fig. 2. Ilé-Ifẹ̀ palace servants at Ọbàtálá's shrine (Photo: Jacob Olúpọ̀nà)

marè's creative and spiritual power – and symbol of his authority as well – was transformed into the environment, the created space, vegetation, land materials, rivers, valleys, and trees. Through the dissemination of this potent force, special places were infused with sacred power. As the primordial gods and spirits, sixteen in number, descended into the world, they took their abodes in these special places, and, henceforth, miraculous occurrences began to take place there. Limited by the length of this essay, I cannot describe the numerous myths associated with the descendants of these gods, referred to as Òrìṣà afẹ̀wọ̀nrọ̀ – those who descended with the primordial chain – the cosmos, and the experience of space and place.

THE COSMOS AND THE EXPERIENCE OF SPACE AND PLACE

In Yorùbá imagination, the cosmos is often described and explained in metaphors of place, structure, spatial dimensions, and orientation. Ilé-Ifẹ̀, the city where creation took place, literally means "an expansive land." It is also described as the place where the day dawns (níbi ojú ti mọ́ wa). Ilé-Ifẹ̀ is the center from whence the inhabitants of the world first viewed daylight. The earth was conceived as highly expansive, in no way spatially confined. The structure of the Yorùbá universe is three-tiered. The highest and first pole of the cosmic universe is ọ̀run, the sky (heaven), the location and inhabited realm of Olódùmarè, the Supreme God, and some of the lesser gods, or Òrìṣà, and other spirits (imolè or ẹbọra). No human is directly concerned with the affairs of heaven (ìṣe ọ̀run). The second and middle pole (ayé) is the center of the cosmos and the inhabited place of the living and of some divinities and spirits. It is the vitalizing center of the world and the point at which all the cosmic forces and power in the three tiers intersect.[15] The third layer, ilẹ̀, the underworld, is the opposite of the sky; it is the place of the dead. Ilẹ̀ is personified by the female earth deity, regarded as the source of creative and generative power of fecundity, exemplifying moral aptitude and justice, and as the ultimate judge and adjudicator in human affairs. She also represents the idea of death as the end product of human life. When we die, she takes us into her body.[16] Although the Yorùbá creation story presents a vertically structured, three-tiered sphere – sky, world, and underworld (the earth) – each sphere also consists of a horizontal dimension that contains its own

inhabitants, gods, mortals, and demons (ajogun). Where they live determines the extent of sacred powers entrusted to them. For example, in addition to being the habitat of Olódùmarè and some divinities, ọ̀run, the
sky, is the space in which the sun, moon, and stars live and act. The
Yorùbá draw heavily on celestial metaphors to convey experiences of humans and, in fact, to effect potent action through sacred words and images. The sun and the moon are viewed as two opposing but necessary
pairs. The rising sun signals the dawn of a new day (àtiwáyé ọjọ́) and is
portrayed as the arrival into the world of new beings. However, simultaneously, this invocation, àtiwáyé ọjọ́, carries the divine command that the
moon must disappear before the arrival of the new day, represented by
the sun (ọjọ́ ki mọ́lè rí òṣùpá). Observation of the movement of the sun
and the moon is often rendered in proverbs. In a more elaborate ritual
context like Ifá divination performance, the opening ritual invocation to
Ifá divination is a prayer-poem addressed to relevant cosmic powers. It
reads:

Iwájú ọpọ́ń	The front of Ifá
Ẹ̀yìn ọpọ́ń	The back of Ifá
Olùbúlotún	The right side of Ifá
Olùmọ̀ràn losì	The all-knowing on the left
Arin ọpọ́ń	The center of Ifá
Òde ọ̀run	The center of heaven
Àtiwáyé ọjọ́	The dawn of the day
Àtiwọ̀ ọ̀run	The setting of the sun
M'áfìbi pere	Do not say it is good when indeed it is bad
M'áfìre pebi	Do not say it is bad when it is good
Máfòlòlò fohùn	Do not speak in a deceitful voice

The diviner's prayer represents a request to Ifá to guide his consulta-
tion in the right path so that unequivocal truth may emerge. By his invo-
cations, the diviner symbolically dramatizes the creation of the cosmos.
The metaphor for the first setting of the sun is particularly significant. At
the center of the divination technique is the idea that the universe and
the events therein are guarded by spiritual and temporal analogies to life.
Ifá is thus the regulator of events in the universe (agbáyégún). Note also
that the divination performance refers to the four cardinal points of the

universe, plus the center – the fifth and focal point. The five important axes of powers are replicated on the Ifá divination tray (*ọpọ́n Ifá*). The divination tray, usually a carved wooden structure, represents the universe (*ayé*). This circular tray is a replica or, in James Livingston's words, a "reproduction, on the human scale, of the cosmos or of Creation itself. It is an *imago mundi*, an image of the original world order."[17]

At times in the course of divination, the *babaláwo* (the Ifá priest) may draw the axes in the yellow powder on the Ifá tray, indicating the connection between the four cardinal points and the center. The center of the divining tray (*arin ọpọ́n*) is the link to the center of heaven (*ìta ọ̀run*), the abode of Olódùmarè and the storehouse of sacred knowledge required to unravel the secret surrounding the client's inquiry, especially in case of sickness, when the *babaláwo* assumes that hidden spiritual forces are behind his client's ailment. The visible sign of touching the four corners and

Fig. 3. Ifá divination session, with tray (Photo: Jacob Olúpọ̀nà)

the center of the tray with the divination chain, or ọpẹlẹ, represents an intricate religious symbolism. By this ritual act, the tray becomes the earthly sacred center from which the diviner makes a connection with the heavenly center (ìta ọrun) – the ultimate place of Ifá's àṣe (healing power) and the individual client's orí (personal destiny). While the Yorùbá recognize that Ifá inhabits the earthly cosmos, his ability to commune with the beings of heaven (ará ọrun) makes divination practice possible. Hence, Ifá also is called agbáyé mọ̀ṣe ọrun ("he who lives on the earth and knows the feats of heaven").

A GEOGRAPHY OF YORÙBÁ SACRED SPACE: CREATION AND THE COSMOS

Within each horizontal cosmic sphere, several activities take place between the tiers. Vertical relationships are established that connect one sphere to the other through the creation process begun in the first sphere, the sky-heaven, the abode of the Supreme God. With the formation of the other two spheres (the world and the earth's underworld), a vertical relationship is established between the three spheres. Olórun, or Olódùmarè (the Supreme Being), controls events in the first sphere, which is also the place of the creation of humans, where Ọbàtálà, the senior-most deity, fashions physical human forms from heaven's clay. Once fashioned and provided with the breath of life, humans depart to take their destiny (orí inú) from the home of Àjàlá, the custodian of destiny. The spirit nature of the human person carrys the calabash of fate (igbá ìwà), which he or she then drops at the threshold of heaven, crosses the river of forgetfulness, and enters the world of the living, where the individual is born as a baby.

Except for the Supreme Being, who maintains his silence after the world has been created, the gods and spirits dwelling in heaven are actively connected with the living on earth. After creation, a group of sixteen immortal gods descend into the world through a chain to take charge of different ministries on earth. Ògún, god of iron and war, leads the way with his cutlass, clearing a path in the world. Ọ̀ṣun, goddess of cool water and the only female deity, follows, as does Ṣàngó, god of thunder and lightning, and Ifá, or Ọ̀rúnmìlà, god of divination and counselor of the gods and humans. Other deities in charge of various human activities and of geographic and physical features also follow until all – agricultural fields, rivers, mountains, and forests – are inhabited by one deity or another. There are deities associated with specific locations and places, such as Ajé, goddess of wealth and prosperity, who is in charge of the market economy, and Ọ̀sanyìn, in charge of herbal medicine. Of the 201 or 401 deities, almost all have a department to control or a function to perform in the world. Likewise, there is no natural phenomena that lacks signifiers of the sacred in the Yorùbá imagination: rain, rainbow, thunder, storm, and wind are interpreted as heavenly forces.

Growing up in a traditional Yorùbá town, I experienced several of these phenomena. Children were encouraged to reflect on these natural phenomena in riddles. For example, an elder may ask, "What is a long thin rod that touches heaven and earth?" (*ọ̀pá tẹ́rẹ́ ó kan lẹ̀, o kan ọ̀runlọ?*) We answered, "rain." The experience of the rainbow on a wet rainy day indicates that Èṣùmàrè, a deity of multiple colors, is drinking water from a riverbank close by. The appearance of a new moon is always welcomed as a favorable time to say one's prayer that the new moon may bestow blessings upon an individual (*oṣù ko lé ire símilára o*). This is a prayer for good luck and blessings. The new moon is also a sign that the mentally ill may become more agitated than usual and a warning to avoid them. We all saw how unusually bright the moon was in December 1999, in California, an indication that a new millennium was about to begin. Several places became imbued with sacred qualities either because the descending gods made these places their abode or because certain "miraculous" events occurred there. While some gods and spirits found their abodes on mountains and hills, others preferred the deep sea and large rivers.

The world (*Ilé-ayé*), the second sphere, is a complex universe. It encompasses both space and habitat. The Yorùbá worldview emphasizes that the central prayer or request from Òrìṣà is for a devotee to have a peaceful existence in one's space and abode (*kí a wà láyé, kí a wà laaye wa*). Within the second-sphere world lie cultivated lands, towns and cities, forests and vegetation. (I will discuss the significance of Ilé-Ifẹ̀ as the sacred city par excellence of the second sphere in a later part of this paper.)

Yorùbá towns and cities are regarded as sacred enclaves for inhabitants of the world (*ayé*). Since early times, most cities and towns were walled off to protect inhabitants from outside intruders and evil spirits. City gates and entrances are not mere passages but thresholds distinguishing people of the city from those of the forest outside. City gates are sites of magical objects and shrines, where Èṣù, gatekeeper god and divine police-man, filters out evil spirits and neutralizes the power of malevolent magic and medicine. Èṣù's protective role is very important for the community, earning him the honorific of Ọláìlú (prosperity or honor of the city). Para-doxically, oníbodè (gatekeepers) who operate city gates are often notori-ous ex-convicts on parole, whose immense physical presence repels in-truders. The famous Bodè Lálúpọn (Lálúpọn Gate) in old Ìbàdàn territory was filled with remarkable stories. Even ordinary events, such as the daily movement of Ìbàdàn's inhabitants to and from the city, often generate profound episodes of symbolic and tangible significance.

A legend has it that at Bodè Lálúpọn, a conflict between the oníbodè (gatekeeper) and a drummer coming from the city outskirts generated a mythical episode of symbolic and cultural importance. According to the legend, the drummer approached the gate playing the talking drum within earshot of Lálúpọn's gatekeeper. As the drummer approached, suddenly the gatekeeper attacked and beat him severely. City dwellers who knew the drummer intervened, and the gatekeeper was asked why he beat this drummer. The gatekeeper replied that the talking drum sent out insulting, offensive remarks. The gatekeeper heard the drum's mes-

Fig. 4. Shrine to Èṣù in Ilé-Ifẹ̀ (Photo: Jacob Olúpọ̀nà)

sage as, "Look at the mouth of chimpanzee, look at the mouth of ògé (a bird), and look at the mouth of the gatekeeper of Lálúpọn." However, the drummer explained he had merely drummed, "I dined with chimpanzee, I dined with the great bird, and I dined with the great gatekeeper of Lálúpọn." The different interpretation of the message results from its similar sound and rhythm. From the legend of Lálúpọn Gate came the Yorùbá proverb *Kò sí ẹnití ó mọ èdè àyàn, àfi ẹnití o mú òpá ẹ lọ́wọ́*, "No one, other than the drummer, can interpret the talking drum." The legend reminds us that the same drum can produce two opposing meanings: one positive, the other negative.

At the city gate lies a transitional point between the city and the outside forest, a multidimensionality of cultures. Beyond this threshold is the forest zone outside the vicinity of the city. The forest represents the abode of spirits, demons, ghosts, dangerous animals, and wild plants and trees. One need only read D. O. Fágúnwà's novel, *Forest of a Thousand Demons: A Hunter's Saga*, to appreciate the significance of the forest in Yorùbá imagination.[18] Only medicine men, brave hunters who are fortified to withstand the possible dangers of the forest's spiritual powers, and ghosts dare enter the forest. Stories of encounters with ghosts, spirits disguised as humans, and animal ghosts with messages to loved ones abound in Yorùbá narratives.

A sizable forest located near a city is often designated as a sacred forest (*Igbó Orò*), occasionally a place where various cult groups meet. The Òsùgbó or Ògbóni secret society, or ancestral masquerades, perform religious activities in such a forest. In the past, the sacred forest has served as the place of public executions. A section of forest may be demarcated for burial of victims of a horrific death, such as from small pox epidemics.

THE CITY AS PLACE AND HOME

I would like now to examine the meaning, images, and spatial orientation of the Yorùbá city, and specifically the most sacred city, Ilé-Ifẹ̀, the place where the world was created. Generally, names of Yorùbá cities and towns are prefaced by *ilé*, meaning home, house, land, or earth. Thus, home, land, and territory are one. In Yorùbá ontology, *ilẹ̀* also signifies the final place of rest. In the context of funeral rites after death, to go home is to join one's ancestors in the afterlife and to return to one's place of origin.

Life in this world is symbolized as a journey that ends with a return to one's home – Ayé l'àjò, bí ó tilẹ̀ pẹ́ pẹ́, a o relé, meaning the world is a journey and, no matter how long we stay abroad, we will return home. As Jonathan Smith remarked, there is a logical connection and a relationship between "home place" and "land."[19] In addition, there is a sense in which, for the Yorùbá, the city is both a place and a people: "it was impossible to speak of a city as a place without a people," writes Ray Laurence.[20] The people of the city sustain the ancestors, gods, and land, and the land in return bestows manifold blessings on the people.

In the history of religions, one of the most studied aspects of sacred place is the sacred, holy city and, although the modality varies from place to place, three types are noticeable in world religions. According to Hariva Pedya, places acquire sacredness as a result of historical or mythical circumstances or events, "because either in theory or in practice they were constructed so as to reflect cosmic reality in a kind of microcosm and divine ground."[21] A city may be sacred because it is the home of a shrine, tomb, or holy object.[22]

The Yorùbá regard Ilé-Ifẹ̀ as the most central, potent place, as mother of all cities. It is the place where the structure and meaning of the sacred cosmos was first unraveled. I would like to explore the meaning and significance of Ilé-Ifẹ̀, in the Yorùbá religious experience, and the role this city has played in formatting Yorùbá religious identity and a sense of place in contemporary Yorùbá politics.

In his classic work Olódùmarè: God in Yorùbá Belief, the father of Yorùbá religious studies, Bọ́lájí Ìdòwú, recalls his experience of Ilé-Ifẹ̀ and describes it for younger generations:

> A young person who was lucky enough in those days to be taken by his parents to Ilé-Ifẹ̀ would approach the city with feelings which baffled analysis. He was bound to be assailed on entering the city with successive waves of emotions. He would be almost afraid to look; for at every turn might be walking or lurking, for all he knew, some divinities or ghosts![23]

Ìdòwú further remarked that "It is clear, then, that a modern and new study of the religion of the Yorùbá should centre around Ilé-Ifẹ̀, although the investigator must take account of all the other important religious and civic centres of Yorùbá life."[24] Ìdòwú confirms Wheatley's earlier discovery of the significance of Ilé-Ifè and the Yorùbá city-states as primarily urban in orientation.

THE PLACE MOST HALLOWED: ILÉ-IFÈ, SACRED CITY

Ilé-Ifè, sacred city of the Yorùbá people of West Africa, is obviously quite familiar to Africanists, especially archaeologists and historians. I do not know of any other ancient African city whose artistic traditions and archaeological findings have been more thoroughly studied than this city. Yet, in spite of all the pioneering works, we know very little about the religious and ritual life, the moral order, and the thought systems that give the city its historical significance and its cultural identity as the ceremonial center of the Yorùbá people. We look in vain for works on Ilé-Ifè as a sacred center on a par with many detailed studies on sacred cities and similar urban centers, such as the Mesoamerican sacred city of Teotihuacan in Mexico, the Hindu city of Banares in India, and even the ancient cities of Jerusalem, Mecca, and Rome.

In *The Pivot of the Four Quarters*, Wheatley indicates that no place in Sub-Saharan Africa, other than the southwestern Yorùbá city of Ilé-Ifè, Nigeria, manifests such cosmic meaning and significance. Known as the City of 201 or 401 Gods, Ilé-Ifè represents the architectural foundation of the entire Yorùbá civilization and culture, whose significance goes far beyond the immediate geographical and national boundaries of Nigeria. The religious culture of Ilé-Ifè has influenced the development and growth of new African religious movements as far off as Brazil, the Caribbean, and the United States.

Ilé-Ifè is situated at the geographical center of the Yorùbá city-states. To the west lies Ìbàdàn, the largest city in Sub-Saharan African, and to the east lies Oǹdó, gateway to the eastern Yorùbá city-states. Ilé-Ifè is about two hundred kilometers from Lagos, Nigeria's coastal capital city for over a century. Unlike the political, commercial, and administrative cities of Ìbàdàn and Lagos, contemporary Ilé-Ifè is a ceremonial city par excellence and, like the cities of Banares, Jerusalem, and Mecca, Ilé-Ifè represents in the people's imagination the preeminent sacred place, beyond the secular and profane.

I begin with Ilé-Ifè's various sacred place-names, because epithets often vividly show the significance of sacred cities. Stephen Scully argues in his book *Homer and the Sacred City* that human centers such as Troy are "richly and complexly described through the epithets attached to them."[25] Citing an earlier study by Paolo Vivante, Scully contends, "City epithets, whenever they occur, bring out the essential aesthetics and contextual quality of place names." These epithets serve "as a resource of power and a medium of signification in their own right"; they are "visual and concrete in nature, and thereby evocative of an essential and generic quality" of whatever they qualify.[26]

In the imagination of its inhabitants, Ilé-Ifè is hallowed in sacred Yorùbá names. Ilé-Ifè has been described as *Ifè Oodáyé*, "the expansive space where the world was created," referring to the cosmogonic myth asserting that ritual creation occurred in this very place, and as *Ibi ojú ti mọ wá* ("where the day dawns"). In Yorùbá creation myth, Ilé-Ifè is conceived of as the place where the sun rises and sets, the center of origin of the universe.

If Ilé-Ifè is the city of the source of life, it is, paradoxically, also the city of the dead. The Yorùbá believe that anyone who dies immediately returns to Ilé-Ifè, the place of origin in their pilgrimage to the other world. Several years ago, I was in my own hometown, Uté, in Owo District, a town located at the extreme eastern end of the eastern Yorùbá territory, to conduct research on death in Yorùbá thought. In a most important song during the burial, the deceased is enjoined to "go on the straight road that leads to Ilé-Ifè and not to stray by the wayside" (*Ònà yó r'ufè maya o*). Ilé-Ifè is regarded as the only stopping place before the dead pass into the underworld, so the rite of passage must ensure that the deceased not tarry on the way to the ancient city. In ancient times, it was the practice of those who had lost their loved ones to travel to Ilé-Ifè to see if the deceased could be sighted, to inform them of the cause of their death, in order to avenge a wrongful death or to tell the deceased about their unfinished business on earth.

Ilé-Ifè attained primacy based on it's hallowed status as the source for all the crowned cities (*Ìlú-Aládé*). An important Yorùbá myth refers to the dispersal of Odùduwà's sixteen royal children, who went out from Ilé-Ifè to found new kingdoms. Each was assigned a sacred crown, or *adé*, a symbol of authority. Each was assigned a sacred sword representing the divine power to take possession of new territories. Stories of the origin of several Yorùbá kingdoms are filled with anecdotes of these royal princes' and princesses' encounters as they conquered aboriginal groups in their newfound lands and ruled with the sacred insignia of office, the crown and the sword.

SYMBOLIC CITY STRUCTURE: QUARTERS, COMPOUNDS, AND HOUSES

The structural organization of Ilé-Ifẹ̀, and its special religious, political, and spatial form, symbolizes the sacred cosmology behind the city's origins. The most important section is the center, the Ọọni's palace, or àfin, located in the heart of the five principal quarters constituting the old city of Ilé-Ifẹ̀. All roads leading from these sections converge in front of the palace, called Ẹnu Ọwá, literally, "mouth of the king." (Ọwá, a synonym for ọbà, or king, is more commonly used in eastern Yorùbá towns than in western towns.) Ẹnu Ọwá indicates the place from which the quarters and the intersections emanate from the royal palace, figuratively the "king's mouth," springing out through the city.

Standing on an elevated site, the afin (palace), often called òkè-ilé (the high or big house), is located at the city center. Three major city roads meet and form an intersection in front of the palace, functioning as an oríta (crossroads), an important phenomenon in Yorùbá religious life. Oríta are not mere crossroads, but represent ritually potent spaces in which sacrifices may be offered to spirits or evil forces (ajogun). Oríta are auspicious places where messages may be conveyed to witches, wizards, and spirit people of the underworld or heaven. The royal palace is protected by the city's concentric layout around its center. As one moves from outermost to innermost circles, degrees of power and sacredness increase. Located close to the palace are the sacred precincts that cradle the three most important ritual centers in the city: the grove, shrine, and temple.

The three sacred precincts are representative: 1) the grove of Odùduwà, cultural hero and founder of the city; 2) Òkè m'ògún, the shrine and hill of Ogun, warrior god, patron deity of the sacred kingship; and 3) Òkè Ìtasẹ̀, Ifá hill and temple, abode of Àràbà Àgbáyé, chief diviner of the universe. Sacred sites of Yorùbá cities are determined by the divination process. Each principal city underwent a divination "corpus" to determine the best site for its origin and growth (*odù tí o tẹ Ìlú dó*). When I asked one of my consultants to name the *odù* on which Ilé-Ifẹ̀ was founded, he exclaimed in surprise, saying that all sixteen principal *odù* talk about the city's origin, an indication that this city is greater than any other city in Yorùbá territory.

SACRED SPACE AND SOCIAL ORDER: IDENTITY, NATIONALISM, AND PLACE

I turn now to the significance of place for nationalism and identity construction in contemporary Yorùbá society. One weak spot in the history of religions is the general lack of in-depth analysis of the relationship between religious phenomena and the social order within which these phenomena exist. The danger of overemphasizing the social context of religion at the expense of the phenomenon itself has encouraged many to avoid probing into the possible social consequences of religious behavior. If historians of religions were to take more seriously Peter Berger's dictum for analyzing religious phenomenon – that we view it in terms of its origin, functions, and intrinsic and substantive value – we would produce a more rounded interpretation of religion that does not privilege one aspect at the expense of the other. Recently, Roger Friedland and Richard Hecht have contended that there is a strong connection between "the construction of sacred space and the social organization of power," and that "ultimately, an adequate theory of sacred places must take cognizance of the political dynamics that play a key role in how it is appreciated, controlled, interpreted, and contested."[27] According to these two authors, "Because they undergird identities and ethical commitments, because they galvanize the deepest emotions and attachments, material and symbolic control over the most central sacred places are sources of enormous social power."[28] One significant place of control is the homeland.

I will examine the role of the homeland and territoriality in the construction of ethnic nationalism, patriotism, and community identity among the Yorùbá. By nationalism, I refer not to the contemporary nation-state context (Nigeria), but to the Yorùbá nation as a cultural group with a homeland, a language, a religion, and a shared culture.[29]

Three related themes should be considered in a template for understanding how sacred cities function in the context of modern nationalism. First, Ilé-Ifẹ̀, as a hallowed land of religious and cultural traditions, was used to mobilize the Yorùbá as a unified patriotic and nationalist group. Second, symbols of sacred place were used in the development of a homeland of subcultural identities and to galvanize the Yorùbá community into a patriotic and national group. Third, the Yorùbá mark their boundaries of sacred space in ritual and ceremonial contexts, which Clifford Geertz calls the rituals of "hallowing the land."[30]

SACRED ILÉ-IFẸ̀ AND THE POLITICS OF PLACE

The study and understanding of sacred place in Yorùbá religious experience may enable us to answer puzzling questions about Yorùbá identity and the role the Yorùbá religion plays in modern Nigerian politics. Why is the ethnicity and ethnic identity of forty million Yorùbá people so strong that it makes their cultural and political life so difficult for outsiders to penetrate? Part of the answer lies in the role that place plays in their political mobilization and the role Ilé-Ifẹ̀, as a centralized sacred place, plays in "creating a religious, communal, and political identity."[31] I contend that Ilé-Ifẹ̀, more than any other Yorùbá city, plays the leading role in forming Yorùbá social and political identity. A second relevant issue, borrowed from Seth Kunin's argument, is that a centralized model of sacred place explains not only identity construction, but also boundary creation.[32] The sacred center defines and delineates "the quality of space and its opposition to the profane" – that which is outside the boundary of the sacred center. While the boundary is centralized in geographical terms, ultimately it is a *cognitive* boundary, providing a psychological and intellectual diagram of "insiders" and "outsiders" in relationship to a sacred center.[33]

The Yorùbá origin myth discussed above is normally followed by another equally powerful myth: that of the dispersion, migration, and odyssey of the children of Odùduwà, who left the sacred city of Ilé-Ifẹ̀ to conquer, inhabit, and establish new dynasties and new cities and towns. With this odyssey, new city-states, such as Oǹdó, Ọ̀wọ̀, Benin, Adó Èkìtì, Ìjẹbú-òde, Ketu, and Ọ̀yọ́, were created, similar to Ilé-Ifẹ̀. In the context of space and land, the migration myth from Ilé-Ifẹ̀ "provides for a plan of cosmological *relatedness*."[34] Yorùbá historian Adéagbo Akinjọ́gbìn describes this relationship between the Ilé-Ifè center and the new city-states as one based on *ẹbí* ideology, in which a sacred pact is made among semi-autonomous kinship groups in defined territorial boundaries. Sociologist Akínsọlá Akìwọ̀wọ̀ described this phenomenon as the fact of Yorùbá *àjọbí* (principles of kinship and association). Though Ilé-Ifè provides a unifying myth, an equal element of decentralization of sacred space is evident in Yorùbá mythology. Multiplicity of sacred space does not necessarily negate our thesis of a centralized sacred space. I will illustrate the significance of Ilé-Ifè in two case studies: the visit of the Ọọni, paramount ruler of Ilé-Ifè, to Lagos in 1938; and the role that the Odùduwà myth played in the formation of a centralized Yorùbá cultural politics: the formation of Ẹgbẹ́ Ọmọ Odùduwà and its political successor, the Action Group Party.

The unprecedented visit of any Ọọni to Lagos occurred in 1938, the announcement of which sent chills to all the other Yorùbá *ọba*, including the Alafin of Ọ̀yọ́. Before this visit, it was taboo for an Ọọni to leave the city of Ilé-Ifè. The other Yorùbá *ọbà* viewed the announcement of his journey with such great alarm and seriousness that they decided to vacate their palaces and stay outside their city for the duration of his visit, and until they could confirm his safe return. While the Ọọni's visit can be interpreted as a sign of the capitulation of the traditional center and society – Ilé-Ifè – to the new colonial center – Lagos – the visit also signaled a reinvention of tradition.

Under the British system of indirect rule, the colonial government had created a new city legislative council, which was in charge of the affairs of the new region. In 1938, a dispute between two Yorùbá rulers, the Ẹlẹ́pẹ́ of Ẹ̀pẹ́ and the Àkárìgbò of Ìjẹ̀bú Rẹmọ, was referred to the state legislative council for adjudication. The Àkárìgbò protested Ẹlẹ́pẹ́'s wearing a bearded crown, which by tradition could be worn only by an *ọbà* claiming direct descent from Odùduwà, who had been authorized to wear the crown by the Ọọni of Ilé-Ifè. At the suggestion of council members, the Ọọni was invited to Lagos to rule on the matter. Hidden behind a screen (since it was forbidden to behold the face of the Ọọni), the Ọọni answered all the questions the council put to him. The Ọọni denounced the Elẹ́pẹ́, lamenting that if it were the old days, the Ọọni would have summoned the Ẹlẹ́pẹ́ to Ilé-Ifè and had him beheaded. What happened between the Ọọni and the British governor after the meeting must be the subject of another essay. In short, the Ọọni was entertained by the governor, in a private meeting, and upon the Ọọni's safe return to Ilé-Ifẹ̀, the Yorùbá ọbà returned to their palaces. By reinventing the traditional power, the British colonial government was able to wend its way through turbulent issues, such as this dispute between the two rulers. Ilé-Ifẹ̀, the Yorùbá place of origin, played a significant role in this process.

The second case study goes back to the 1940s and 1950s pre-independent era of Yorùbá politics, when new colonial dispensations of power in Nigeria reinforced old ethnic cleavages. Thus, a member of the new educated elite emerged: Chief Ọbafẹmi Awólọ́wọ̀ founded a new political party, the Action Group Party, and clearly gathered the Yorùbá under its banner. He appealed to the sensibilities of the Yorùbá by identifying himself with an already existing cultural and quasi-political group, the Ẹgbẹ́ Ọmọ Odùduwà (Society of the Descendants of Odùduwà). In the Yorùbá origin myth, Ilé-Ifẹ̀ became a powerful symbol in mobilizing the Yorùbá into a new political order. In the Yorùbá imagination, Awólọ́wọ̀ gradually became the reincarnation of Odùduwà, a transformation reflected in the Ifẹ̀ title he bore – Aṣíwájú (leader) of the Yorùbá. A popular song in praise of Awólọ́wọ̀, composed by Herbert Ogunde, a celebrated Yorùbá musician, aptly describes the roles of Ilé-Ifẹ̀ and Awólọ́wọ̀ in this pan-Yorùbá nationalism:

Kini ǹba Siǹ
Bikoṣe Olúwo wa
Awólọ́wọ̀, Ìwọ ni mo jírí loni Ire ǹbámi bọ̀,
Ire owo, Ire ọmọ, Ire alaafia

To whom shall I pay homage [literally, worship] if not Awólọ́wọ̀?
Our great high priest [Olúwo]
You are the one to whom I have come to give praise
[as in propitiation of a deity]
When I pay homage to you, I will receive the blessings of children, wealth, and long life

Implicit in this song of praise is the essence of a Yorùbá religious quest, the desire for and promise of a full life by the Òrìṣà (deity). The subtext is that those who associate themselves with the great Yorùbá political priest will receive from the deity the threefold blessings of life. Awólọ́wọ̀ is referred to as the Ifá great priest (Olúwo), who is powerful enough to unravel the secrets of heaven and provide to his people the promise of good life, represented in the role that the Ilé-Ifẹ̀ senior diviner plays. It is very interesting that the new modern political party, the Action Group headed by Chief Awólọ́wọ̀, was anchored in Odùduwà's myth of creation. When, several years later, a renegade group attempted to challenge the hegemony of the Action Group by setting up a counterpart Yorùbá political group, the NNDP, its own cultural and ideological base was found in its name, Ẹgbẹ́ Ọmọ Ọlọ́fin (Society of the Descendants of Ọlọ́fin). Ọlọ́fin is a synonym for Odùduwà, an indication that there was no way of getting out of the matrix of the Odùduwà/Ọlọ́fin myth of Yorùbá origin that had taken place in the sacred city of Ilé-Ifẹ̀.

While Ilé-Ifẹ̀ provides the pan-Yorùbá ideology for natural unity, other cities and towns that claim their origin from the sacred source have also developed subethnic identities for their inhabitants. In the modern period, at least since the 1990s, Yorùbá towns and cities are succeeding in galvanizing their communities toward social and economic development, following several years of military misrule and neglect. The absence of any meaningful improvement in the welfare of the people has made community projects even more resonant today.[36] The strongest instrument of mobilization is the appeal to symbols of religion and culture, such as myths of the sacred home place and the totemic symbols associated with natural phenomena – rivers, mountains, forest, and trees.

In the construction of the subethnic Yorùbá identity and invocation of city nationalism, the most vital symbols invoked are represented by geographical elements connected to the city origin, totemic objects regarded as the spiritual source connected to Ilé-Ifẹ̀: the Ọ̀sun river goddess in Òsogbo; Òrósùn Hill in Idanre; and Òkè-Ìbàdàn Hill in Ìbàdàn.

As further illustration, the Ẹ̀gbá of Abẹòkúta invokes the Olúmọ tutelary deity, of Olúmọ Hill, as a pivotal symbol of their city, Abẹòkúta, in the following "national" anthem in which they also recall the history of their protection by the mountain deity during the Yorùbá civil war. As one example of this, the Ẹ̀gbá ethnic identity expressed in the following song describes the significance of Olúmọ, a sacred hill, in the Ẹ̀gbá's history and origin:

Hail and rejoice under the Olúmọ Hill, Abẹ̀òkúta,
Land of the Ẹ̀gbá People,
I will never forget you,
I will exult you and embrace you always,
Rejoice as you stand under Olúmọ Hill.

Despite the strong influence of Christian and Muslim fundamental-ism, in almost all Yorùbá cities and towns carefully chosen cultural symbols have assured a dimension of civil religion without any reference to sectarian property. In most places, a particular day is set apart and named after the symbol of community identity. The day is enjoyed as a holiday by the community. It is a day of celebration and of contributions of money for community development projects. Olóròkè Day in Òkè-Igbó, for example, is named after a mountain deity of the same name, and the tutelary deity of the city. The purpose of this day is to cel-ebrate common origins and homeland places tied to religion – cultural symbols of immeasurable value for contemporary political gain.

CONCLUSION

The history and geography of religion provide ample evidence of the ways religious myths, rituals, and symbols sacralize places and territories. Through their religious experiences and expressions the Yorùbá people of southwestern Nigeria have elaborated a special metaphor from their ex-perience of place. This concept or significance of place is not limited to traditional life, but continues to influence their activities in present-day Nigeria, as demonstrated by the evolution of politics and nationalism in southwestern Nigeria.

NOTES

1. Roy A. Rappaport, *Ecology, Meaning, and Religion* (Richmond, Calif.: North Atlantic Books, 1979), 209.

2. Ibid.

3. Mircea Eliade, *The Sacred and the Profane: The Nature of Religion* (San Diego: Harcourt Brace Jovanovich, 1959), 22.

4. Jonathan Z. Smith, *To Take Place: Toward Theory in Ritual* (Chicago: University of Chicago Press, 1987), 14–15.

5. Rappaport, *Ecology, Meaning, and Religion*, 210.

6. T. Sole and K. Wood, "Project of Indigenous Sacred Sites: The New Zealand Experience," in *Aboriginal Involvement in Park and Protected Areas*, ed. Jim Birckhead, Terry De Lacey, and Larajane Smith (Canberra: Aboriginal Studies Press, 1992), 342; quoted in Jane Hubert, "Sacred Beliefs and Beliefs of Sacredness," in *Sacred Sites, Sacred Places*, ed. David L. Carmichael, Jane Hubert, Brian Reeves, and Audhild Schanche (London and New York: Routledge, 1994), 11.

7. Smith, *To Take Place*, 26–29.

8. Seth D. Kunin, *God's Place in the World: Sacred Space and Sacred Place in Judaism* (London and New York: Cassell, 1998), 11.

9. Ibid., 21.

10. Ibid., 22.

11. Hubert, "Sacred Beliefs and Beliefs of Sacredness," 11.

12. Kunin, *God's Place in the World*, 21.

13. Dorothea Theodoratus and Frank LaPena, "Wintu Sacred Geography of Northern California," in *Sacred Sites, Sacred Places*, ed. David L. Carmichael, Jane Hubert, Brian Reeves, and Audhild Schanche (London and New York: Routledge, 1994), 21.

14. G. J. Afọlábí Òjó, *Yoruba Culture: A Geographical Analysis* (Ilé-Ifẹ̀: University of Ifẹ̀ Press, 1967), 194.

15. Issiaka Lalèyê, *La conception de la personne dans la pensée traditionelle Yoruba: Approche phénoménologique* (Berne: Herbert Lang, 1987), 73.

16. Ibid.

17. James C. Livingston, *Anatomy of the Sacred: An Introduction to Religion* (New York: Macmillan, 1989), 56.

18. D. O. Fagunwa, *Forest of a Thousand Demons: A Hunter's Saga*, trans. Wole Soyinke (London: Nelson, 1982).

19. Smith, *To Take Place*, 25–30.

20. Ray Laurence, "Ritual, Landscape, and the Destruction of Place in the Roman Imagination," in *Approaches to the Study of Ritual: Italy and the Ancient Mediterranean*, ed. John B. Wilkins, Accordia Specialist Studies on the Mediter-

ranean, vol. 2 (London: Accordia Research Centre, University of London, 1996), 120.

21. Hariva Pedya, "The Divinity as Place and Time as the Holy Place in Jewish Mysticism," in *Sacred Space: Shrine, City, Land*, ed. Benjamin Z. Kedar and R. J. Zvi Werblowsky (New York: New York University Press, 1998), 11.

22. Ibid.

23. E. Bọ́lájí Ìdòwú, *Olódùmarè: God in Yorùbá Belief* (New York: Original Publications, 1994), 11–12.

24. Ibid., 15.

25. Stephen Scully, *Homer and the Sacred City* (Ithaca, N.Y.: Cornell University press, 1990), 4.

26. Ibid., 73, 72.

27. Roger Friedland and Richard D. Hecht, "The Politics of Sacred Place: Jerusalem's Temple Mount/ *al-haram al sharif*," in *Sacred Places and Profane Spaces: Essays in the Geographics of Judaism, Christianity, and Islam*, ed. Jamie Scott and Paul Simpson-Honsley (New York: Greenwood Press, 1991), 28.

28. Ibid., 23.

29. Hedva Ben-Israel, "Hallowed Land in the Theory and Practice of Modern Nationalism," in Benjamin Z. Kedar and R. J. Zwi Werblowsky, eds., *Sacred Space: Shrine, City, Land* (New York: New York University Press, 1998), 282.

30. Ibid., 279.

31. Kunin, *God's Place in the World*, 26.

32. Ibid.

33. Ibid., 27.

34. Tony Swain and Garry W. Trompf, *The Religions of Oceania* (London and New York: Routledge, 1995), 24.

35. Akínsọlá Akìwọ̀wọ̀, personal communication.

36. Lillian Trager, *Yoruba Hometowns: Community, Identity, and Development in Nigeria* (Boulder, Colo.: Lynn Rienner Publishers, 2001).

WHO IS HILDEGARD?
WHERE IS SHE – ON HEAVEN?

MARY GERHART

INTRODUCTION

My first encounter with Hildegard came about indirectly. In the course of doing research for my book *Genre Choices, Gender Questions*, I noticed that the abundant new publications on the history of monasteries included little on the history of women's monasteries. Indeed, until this century most histories of monasticism took no notice of women's monasteries whatever: even studies described as "definitive" work on monastic life ignored women's monasteries. The nadir of neglect may have been in the 1950s when J. G. Davies stated that he did not include women in his study of early Christianity because there was nothing to be learned from women's lives that was not already well known from studies of men's. He wrote: "Women's lives were sufficiently unvaried to be incapable of sustained and detailed description." Even texts with details are useless, he thought, because they merely replicate the details of monks "which were vividly documented and well preserved."[1] Today, women's monasteries are often treated as afterthoughts in an appendix, as in the case in Chris Hellier's *Monasteries of Greece*. Sacheverrell Sitwell, in his book on English monasteries, *Monks, Nuns, and Monasteries*, does include women's monasteries, but nothing about the people who lived there.[2] As a result, connections between the lives of women and the monasteries they lived in are yet to be made.

I also found that the most promising sources for discovering the places where women like Hildegard built monasteries are also indirect – an outgrowth of the resurgence of interest in the writings of and about women by women mystics in the Middle Ages. The first clue to place can usually be found in a woman's name: for example, Gertrude of *Helfta* or Mechtilde of *Magdeburg*. Biographers, commentators, and the texts themselves also regularly include geographical information. Anthologies of women mystics' writings (often arranged by country of birth) are helpful since the location of physical birth and the sites of monastic life in those times were usually proximate. Anyone interested today in doing on-site studies of the houses of individual medieval women writers or of monasticism that is gender inclusive can find clues for the reconstruction of lives and places – clues that even thirty years ago were assumed either not to exist or to be inconsequential.

In this project I started with Hildegard of *Bingen*, one of only three women of the twelfth century whose writings are extant.[3] Barbara Newman noticed that the first translations of Hildegard's work, from medieval Latin into German, were done in 1929 for the 750th anniversary of her death and that, as recently as 1968, few medievalists would recognize her name.[4]

What began as a feminist concern – namely, a concern for equal treatment of women in the scholarly history of monasteries – quickly became for me an intriguing hermeneutical challenge: Who was Hildegard? What was she? Where did she become what she was? These questions might seem to be straightforward and to require straightforward answers. But what is one to do with problems of immensely difficult translation? Hildegard frequently commented on her lack of scholarly training, yet in the course of her lifetime she had five secretaries (at one time, two simultaneously). What should be done with cracking the code to the private language in two of her minor writings?[5] If this private language was just an amusing parlor game, as Sabina Flanagan hypothesizes, there may be little to understand in what has been thought to be a significant datum in earlier studies of Hildegard.[6] On the other hand, if private language is what she refers to in the *Book of the Rewards of Life*[7] as "the symphony of the harmony of Heavenly revelations, and an unknown language with letters," a problem remains to be solved.

What *is* there to be understood? And what do we even mean by that question? If we mean, what evidence of her life and activities is available, we can point to the 481-page, double-columned, 12 x 18 inch, 33-pound, parchment Riesen Kodex, that includes all her work except her scientific writings.[8] Kept in Wiesbaden, this manuscript seems to have been compiled in support of her nomination for canonization a decade after her death, at age eighty-two, in 1179.[9] A request for further documentation from the canonization commission in Rome in the first half of the thirteenth century seems not to have been answered – either that, or the answer was lost, or the matter was dropped. In any event, it is recorded that the Curia did not receive the amended version drawn up to answer further questions. By the fourteenth century, however, martyrologies included her name and feast day, and "express permission for her 'solemn and public cult' is found in an indulgence from John XXII dated from Avignon in 1324."[10] She is also included in Baronius's *Roman Martyrology* of the sixteenth century.

The rediscovery of Hildegard in the twentieth century revealed her to be a major figure in the 1100s. Referred to as the "Sibyl of the Rhine" by her contemporaries, she had correspondence of consequence with Frederick Barbarossa, who became king of Germany in 1152 (and Holy Roman Emperor in 1155). She also corresponded with many political and ecclesiastical leaders of her time, including four popes. That copies of her work circulated during her lifetime is evidence of unusual interest in what she had to say. The existence of letters asking her for her sermons[11] suggests that her calls for reform were discussed beyond the immediate audience to whom they were delivered and were used as a tool for reform by her contemporaries. However, the interest that her work generated in her lifetime has been surpassed since the 1930s by that of people whose interests range widely (monastics, spirituality-seekers, historians, scientists, musicians), from those who find her extraordinary to others like Charles Singer who, writing in the tradition William James called "medical materialism," attribute her visions to migraine headaches.[12]

Let us ask the question again: What is to be understood? We suddenly notice that the verb tense has both shifted and been augmented: "Who *was* Hildegard in her lifetime?" has become "Who *is* the Hildegard we can know through our investigation of sources, through our consideration of different interpretations of her texts, and through reflection on our own questions?" The attempt to recover Hildegard is hermeneutical in the sense that the horizons (or understandings) of the interpreter as well as that of the object of interpretation need to be made explicit.

And now the immensity of this hermeneutical task begins to be perceived. The nineteenth-century founders of general hermeneutics thought that the job of interpretation was to empathize with the mind of the author. By contrast, contemporary hermeneutical theorists see the work of interpretation as a reconstruction of the data "in front of the text."[13] Although it is possible to construe data as distanced from geographical, historical, and biological factors, I decided to pursue some semblance of immediacy by paying attention to what used to be called, in literary criticism, "local color" – data in the text formerly overlooked or ignored, data that raise new questions addressed to the text by the reader and to the reader by the text. In effect, I asked, "What would a sense of *place* add to Hildegard understood as a phenomenon to be reconstructed?"

I began by focusing on Hildegard's idea of Heaven as the most complex treatment of place in her work. Immediately, the hermeneutical dimensions of this issue required that I treat Hildegard as a "what" in addition to a "who" and that I treat Heaven as a "where" in relation to what her texts and residences suggest today – this in addition to their potential historical and theological meanings. What results is the "manufacture" of Hildegard with a broad method of interpretation.

Consider the relations of Hildegard's five major texts,[14] first to the places where she lived and worked, and then to an experience of visiting three of those places: the first, Disibodenberg (also known as the Monastery of St. Disibod, on the site of the enclosure where she went to live as a child); the second, at Bingen-Brücke (the site of the Rupertsberg Monastery whose construction she herself supervised and moved into with her sisters in 1150); and the third, at Eibingen on the eastern bank of the Rhine, the site of another monastery, the Eibingen, founded in 1165 (Hildegard crossed the Rhine twice weekly to visit the Eibingen). In this narrative another site, Rüdesheim – a twentieth-century Benedictine monastery with no connection to the original sites but often mistakenly referred to in the literature as the Abbey of St. Hildegard at Eibingen – is actually a mile or so east of the original Eibingen Monastery.

In the case of each of the following texts, the visionary writings are reported as having been written after the visions had been completed.[15]

The five texts are:

First, *The Scivias*, a book of twenty-six visions, sometimes referred to as a "theological summa,"[16] written between 1141 and 1151 at Disibodenberg when Hildegard was in her forties. Many scholars take the title to be an abbreviation for *Scito vias Domini*. The title has been translated as either *Know the Ways of the Lord* or *The Ways of the Lord*. In the first translation, "scivias" is treated as an imperative; the second is merely an abbreviation of the first. Besides being translated as either an imperative grammatical form or an indicative (i.e., "You know the ways of the Lord"), it could also be translated appropriately as a subjunctive "Would that you knew . . . ," or what we might call a polite imperative, "May you know the ways of the Lord."

Second, *Causes and Cures*, a book of medical care appropriate for the life cycle within a theological framework, written between 1151 and 1158 at the Rupertsberg when Hildegard was in her fifties.

Third, *The Book of the Rewards of Life* (alternatively translated as *The Book of Life's Merits*), a book of astute psychological observations in a cosmological context on the relationships between moral weaknesses and virtues, based on one vision that Hildegard worked on for five years, in her early sixties, between 1158 and 1163, also at the Rupertsberg.

Fourth, *The Book of Divine Works*, an encyclopedic cosmology based on ten visions, written in her late sixties and early seventies at the Rupertsberg between 1163 and 1174.

And finally, fifth, a musical composition from *The Symphonia*, a collection of her musical works, composed as liturgies from 1140 on, when Hildegard was in her forties through seventies (wherever she was residing at the time), and bound in two different collections (1175 and 1180), one just before and one just after her death.

What began for me as a fascination with a major theologian, composer, prophet, visionary, and possibly artist of the twelfth century turned into a wrestling match with a huge bin of gnarled and knotted twine. However much I read, I had a sense that mere information was not enough. Neither Hildegard's biography nor her cosmology lends itself to a straightforward textual analysis: In order to retrieve pre-critical beliefs of nine hundred years ago – beliefs vastly different from ours today – I found that I needed a sense of place in order to reconstruct information within my own mind-space. Hildegard's thought differentiates "scientific" from "religious" fields of meanings only descriptively. Her cosmology does not differentiate clearly among the terms Earth/Heaven and Earth/Hell, as we have come to expect. Since the early twentieth century, most of us allow the demythologization project of Rudolf Bultmann unhesitatingly to determine our own understanding of those terms, simply eliminating Heaven and Hell and leaving Earth a single story.

Furthermore, Hildegard challenges any merely evolutionary feminist understanding of her achievements by having led an extraordinarily well-documented intellectual life concurrent with the founding of most universities. At the University of Salerno, one of the first universities to be founded, only one woman, an herbalist, had professorial status. Hildegard's multifaceted public life suggests a certain plasticity of gender restraints previous to the founding of universities. Within a few centuries the probability of there being a woman such as Hildegard was much diminished. Nevertheless, in dealing with the historical dimensions of both the demythologization of Heaven and Hildegard's place in the history of thought, I have found helpful Marymay Downing's hypothesis (created while she was working on goddess religions of Crete) that belief, religious or otherwise, at any given time in the past "may have been . . . in quite simple terms, or in theologically complex and profound terms, and the full range in between as well, just as religious beliefs vary among individuals, and over an individual's lifetime."[17] I take this hypothesis to refer not only to formally expressed objectifications of beliefs – or, if you will, doctrine – but to the potential tension between all stated beliefs and recorded actions.

In what follows, I will first describe my experience of Hildegard's places. I will then reflect on representative uses of the term "Heaven" from her major writings in order to reconstruct three contexts privileged in her use of the term – in her accounts of her visions, in her cosmology, and in her songs for liturgies. Each of these three contexts lends itself to a particular kind of understanding, the first two to metaphorical and analogical understanding, respectively. For the third context, I will comment on a recording of one of the antiphons she composed for St. Disibod's feast day in order to enable us to intuit how liturgical music – for her and for us – might appropriate the experience of Heaven as an ecstatic sense of the whole.

EXPERIENCING THE PLACES

The first problem with any place is finding it. In December 1995 I flew to Germany to retrieve what I could of two monasteries of women, one at Bingen (that expanded into four) and one at Helfta – a story for another day.[18]

After landing at Frankfurt, I picked up a rental car and headed for Bingen, forty kilometers to the southwest on the west bank of the Rhine. What should have been a half-hour drive took three times as long since, a little dazed from jet lag, I turned off the Autobahn too soon. The information center in Bingen found me a room in a pension in Binger-Brücke, across the bridge over the Nähe. Later that day I discovered that the Rupertsberg, the monastery founded by Hildegard after she left Disibodenberg, had been located at the site of an office furniture store just a few blocks from my room. (The place reminded me that Elizabeth Cady Stanton's home in Seneca Falls, New York, lay under a laundry until its restoration in the 1980s.) The only existing sketch of the Rupertsberg appears in the background of a painting of the Madonna by Grünewald.[19] But the details – for example, that the monastery, built between 1250 and 1252, had running water – are known only from the writings of Hildegard and others.

The first place was Disibodenberg, just barely legible on my detailed map of the Rhineland. And so it came to pass that I found myself the next morning driving south, first on #42, a two-lane highway, and then on gravel roads largely unmarked except for small-town destinations. Finally, I was close enough to inquire at an inn, where a clutch of midday wine-tasters told me – syncopated, like a chorus – to turn left after crossing the bridge down the road and to follow the signs.

The ruins of the Disibodenberg are today managed by a winery that owns the land and surrounding vineyards. A one-lane road leads to the winery. Passing a car coming from the opposite direction is a risky venture: drivers on the inside seek indentations in the hill to pause, while those passing in the outer lane sense the danger of slipping off the cliff and into the Nähe. Across from the parking lot was a recently erected gate with a box stating a DM 3 entrance and tour fee. Since this was early winter and no other tourists were in sight, I made the quarter-mile climb of the thirty-some degree incline alone.

As I approached the summit, I felt a foggy damp cold enveloping the

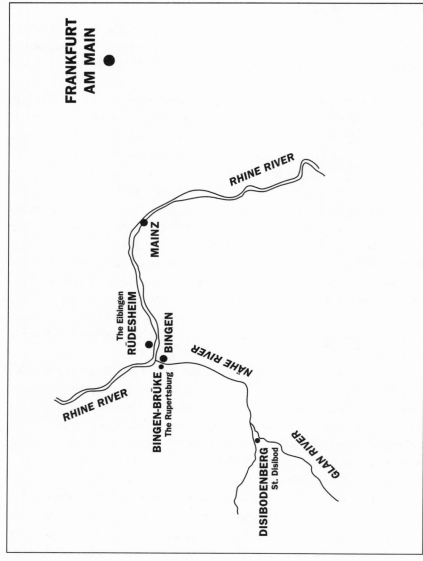

Fig. 1. The three monasteries where Hildegard of Bingen lived: Disibodenberg, Bingen-Brüke, and Rüdesheim

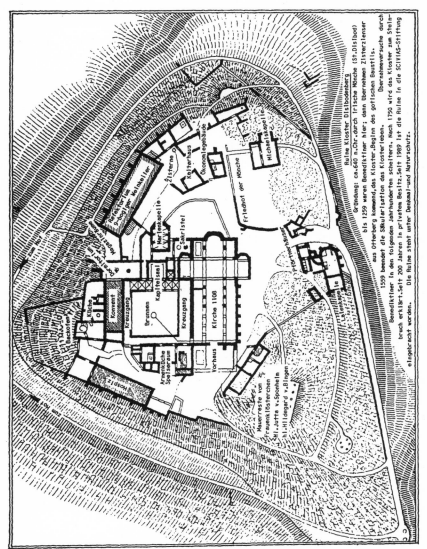

Fig. 2. Diagram on site of ruins of St. Disibod Monastery, from photograph taken November 1998 (Photo: Mary Gerhart)

hill. The ruins were hidden by trees until I came upon them. Tall and spectral in the mist, the walls that remain were much larger and more complete than I had expected. The fog made it easy to imagine people eating in the refectory and gliding from one building to another. The first biography of Hildegard, by Gottfried of Disibodenberg and Theodoric of Echternach (a redaction of several texts completed between 1181 and 1187), states that Disibodenberg was a hermitage to which Hildegard had come with another girl, in 1106, when she was eight years old. Here she joined Jutta of Sponheim who, with a group of male hermits, lived on this hill originally founded by a ninth-century Irish monk named Disibod. In the introduction to her *Hildegard of Bingen, On Natural Philosophy and Medicine*, Margret Berger thinks it more likely that Jutta – who according to recent research turns out to be only six years older than Hildegard – began to be educated for monastic life in her own home in Sponheim together with Hildegard and an unnamed girl Hildegard's age. Whatever was the case, it was not until the double monastery was completed in 1108 that the women and men began to live by the Rule of St. Benedict. When Jutta died, Hildegard was elected abbess (some think only magister, not abbess) of the women's community to continue the spiritual and cultural education of young women of nobility (as was Hildegard herself).

I climbed what remained of the chapel steps. An excavation on the right contained a pile of stones, arranged by size; on the left, a pile of branches recently cut. I climbed down about six feet and walked the length of the foundation, all the while imagining processions that had wended here and now faded in the mist. Thanks to a framed sketch erected near the refectory, I could identify other buildings (see fig. 2). The layout of this "double" monastery – kitchen, bakery, women's dormitories, men's dormitories, library, barn, alms-kitchen, warming-room, storeroom, hostel, wine-pressing room, and wine cellar – is clearly discernible. (Notice the so-called enclosure where some commentators think Jutta and her early community lived.) I was struck by the size and the completeness of the complex. But, in addition, I felt a presence that was so much more than woods and stone. No birds sang and, except for the rustling of leaves, all was silence. All traces of the intervening nine centuries – vanished.

Back at the winery I rang a large bell and was admitted to a museum that had separate rooms for viticulture and monastic history. There I

Fig. 3. Disibodenberg Monastery in the mist (Photo: Mary Gerhart)

found roughly hewn stone sculptures and bas-reliefs – strikingly medieval and different from others I have seen – as well as archaeological documents on the history of the buildings.

In retrospect, I realize how much was left to the imagination: the details of where and how Hildegard composed the *Scivias*, her first book, and how she worked with her secretaries, the monk Volmar, and her beloved companion Richardis von Stade, what communal practices the monks and the nuns with their abbess Jutta carried out before they adopted the Rule of St. Benedict. And, even further back, how the Irish monk Disibod had come to choose this piece of land. On these questions, the locus genii was silent. Remembering the mist brings to mind one of the word's earliest meanings, now archaic – "mystery, the unfathomable." But I also recall that Hildegard's reasons for asking for permission of the ecclesiastical authorities to leave Disibodenberg were unfathomable to many of her contemporaries. Hildegard's desire to build a separate monastery, the Rupertsberg, for women must have been at least as complex as any of the factors known to us. That she was astute economically is shown in a letter to her abbot, reminding him that if he were to keep her community at Disibodenberg because of income from their dowries, the restraint was a form of usury, and punishable!

After I returned to Bingen I asked myself: Why build a new monastery in a much more difficult environment? What did it take for Hildegard and her companions to separate from the monks with whom they had inaugurated a double monastery at Disibodenberg? We know that deprivations endured by the Rupertsberg community were a probable cause for an early unexpected departure of some of her companions. We also know that the newly located community grew so rapidly that fifteen years after the building of the Rupertsberg Hildegard decided to move once more.

The next day the car ferry took me across the Rhine from Bingen to Rüdesheim where, rather than building anew, Hildegard had acquired a former Augustinian monastery for her third monastic home, Eibingen. The physical remains of the Eibingen monastery have been incorporated into the local parish church. Although the church was dark on this late winter afternoon, I could see murals representing scenes from Hildegard's life painted on one side of the nave and the little ornate casket, her final place, built into the altar.

Less than a kilometer from the place of the Eibingen church is the

Abbey of St. Hildegard, begun before World War I but not finished until after World War II. There I spoke with Ancilla Ferlings, a Benedictine nun, about visionaries and mystics as they are understood today. She recalled Karl Rahner's dictum that the world will cease to exist unless it becomes more mystical. Even though she emphasized that Benedictines are encouraged to find and develop their own individual spiritual path, she surprised me by saying she thought it more likely that today mystics would live outside rather than inside the cloister.

Other people I talked with told me that current interest in Hildegard began in the United States in 1979 with the 800th anniversary of her death. My innkeeper's name in Bingen-Brücke was Hildegard. Her late husband had given her a medal struck by the government in commemoration of that anniversary. Everyone I talked to welcomed the "interdisciplinary" interest in Hildegard and her writings – from medical science to philology. They spoke with admiration of scholars within religious communities laboriously translating and interpreting difficult medieval manuscripts as well as of New Age enthusiasts who identify with her spirit and, more recently, other scholars interested in one or another aspect of her work, such as her musical composition. In the last five years some eight recordings of her music in radically different styles have hit Platinum on the music ratings.[20] (In 2000, HMV in Harvard Square carried twenty-five different recordings of her work.) I came away stirred by the remnants of the places where she lived and worked, and later – as I began to understand her work better – by the diversity, religious insight, and originality of her writings.

THREE "PLACES" IN WHICH HEAVEN IS MANIFEST

Heaven as Voice: The Metaphorical

The first context for taking up Hildegard's use of the concept of Heaven is in her identification of the source of her visionary understanding as a "voice from Heaven." *Scivias*, her first book, records a most vibrant account of her experience of Heaven as a voice as both an experience of presence and as illumination. Here place is implicated in terms of where she was at a particular time in her life:[21]

It happened that, in the eleven hundred and forty-first year of the Incarnation of the Son of God, Jesus Christ, when I was forty-two years and seven months old, Heaven was opened and a fiery light of exceeding brilliance came and permeated my whole brain, and inflamed my whole heart and my whole breast, not like a burning but like a warming flame, as the sun warms anything its rays touch.

This description of her experience of Heaven is preceded by a description of the circumstances of the vision: ". . . as I was gazing with great fear and trembling attention at a Heavenly vision, I saw a great splendor in which resounded a voice from Heaven, saying to me, 'speak and write these things . . . as you see and hear them on high in the Heavenly places in the wonders of God'" (*Scivias* 59). We know from two of Hildegard's other writings – *Causes and Cures* and *The Rewards of Life* – that the wonders of God constitute an astonishingly detailed universe. But here the wonders are confined to formal scriptural revelation: "And immediately I knew the meaning of the exposition of the Scriptures, . . . though I did not have the interpretation of the words of their texts or the division of the syllables or the knowledge of cases or tenses." And what was this meaning? ". . . I had sensed in myself wonderfully the power and mystery of secret and admirable visions from childhood." Hildegard thus presents her visions as a continuum of experiences since childhood, differing now in her maturity only in that she is ordered to ". . . write, therefore, the things you see and hear" – an order that she refuses to yield to for a long time. Only when strengthened by many illnesses and by the witness of the monk Volmar ("the man she had secretly sought and found") and the nun Richardis von Stade ("a noble maiden of good conduct") did she "set her hand to writing" what she heard and received "in the Heavenly places" ("Declaration," in *Scivias*, 59–61). To the Anglo-American, "place" immediately connotes a geographically determinable space. For Hildegard, who for her adult life had lived only at Disibodenberg, "place" encompasses a specific time in her life and is intimately connected to the two friends who helped her discern what to make of her visions. Hildegard is confirmed in her intense response to the visions.

Of Hildegard's three books written in the form of visions, two contain extended statements describing how the visions came upon her. The first vision, translated as "Declaration: These Are Two Visions Flowing from

Fig. 4. "Cosmic Humanity," an illumination from the *Book of Divine Works* (sometimes called the *Book of Divine Action*), MS 1942, Lucca, Biblioteca Statale. Although the subject of this vision is abstract, Hildegard's vision is of a concrete theological and cosmic location. The divine trinity and the cosmos embrace the human. The seven planets known in her time appear above the human being in a straight line in the outer circle of the "wheel of marvelous appearance." They shine their rays at the animal heads as well as at the human figure, while clouds and watery air moisten the other circles with dampness. In the lower left corner, Hildegard herself is envisioned receiving the vision. (From Schipperges, *The World of Hildegard of Bingen*, p. 75)

God," occurs at the beginning of *Scivias*. The second, called "Foreword" by the editors, occurs at the beginning of the *Book of Divine Works* (see fig. 4). The terms "a voice from Heaven" and "the voice from Heaven" are used several times in both texts. In *Scivias*, Hildegard is formally invoked by the voice from Heaven in the second person as "o fragile human," "o human," and then referred to as "she" and as "the person whom I have chosen" to speak and to write. In this early text, the "voice from Heaven" speaks in the first person pronoun – "I" – only as the agent of Hildegard's bodily illnesses and spiritual purging.

In the *Book of Divine Works*, written twenty-three years later, Hildegard is addressed more intimately as "you" and as "o wretched creature and daughter of much toil." In this later text, the "I" of the "voice from Heaven" seems to be more forthcoming about itself. Hildegard is told to write (but here not to speak), "not as your heart is inclined but rather as my testimony wishes. For I am without any beginning or end of life." Indeed, the voice from Heaven takes on an explicitly cosmic identity: the voice states that the vision is not contrived by any human, but "instead I have established all of it from before the beginning of the world. And just as I knew the human species even before its creation I also saw in advance everything that humanity would need" (*Book of Divine Works*, 5–6). In this later text the personal, with reference to both Hildegard and to the voice of Heaven, seems less circumstantial and more sure of its identity in the larger scheme of reality. Ironically, Hildegard seemingly no longer needs to avoid "arrogance of mind" – a concern she had expressed in the early text.

"Heaven" in the visionary texts is best understood metaphorically, not in the sense of a substitute of one referent for another – but in the strong sense of metaphor in which someone asserts that two things from different fields of meanings are the same.[22] In this case, Heaven (traditionally a state of existence after death for souls who have died after leading good lives) is asserted to be the originating site of an overwhelmingly gracious situation.

In both texts, the term "Heaven" is most likely to occur either in Hildegard's quotation of scripture or in code phrases, such as "Heavenly Father," "secret places in Heaven," and Man's "being lifted up above the heavens." One of the most curious expressions distinguishes between Paradise and Heaven: "Man is tested by every creature, in Paradise, on

Earth, and in Hell, and then he is placed in Heaven" (*Scivias*, 8). The resulting new meaning of Heaven as metaphor is found in the refrain at the beginning of many of the visions in *Scivias*: "And again I heard the voice from Heaven, saying to me: 'The visible and temporal is a manifestation of the invisible and eternal'" (*Scivias*, 94). This claim seems to me to be more one of identity than of likeness.

Her understanding is different from a conventional religious understanding that places Heaven in some kind of afterlife, either in terms of an end-time after Earth "passes away" or at the termination of an individual life. For those who interpret subjectivistically, Heaven is no more than a state of mind for the individual or a set of circumstances (such as economic prosperity, marital bliss) that fulfills the individual's highest aspirations. For the literalist, the origin of Heaven is external to the human situation; for the subjectivist, Heaven is no more than transitory personal experience. Even if these two types in their pure forms are rare, they do locate poles of meaning that are often articulated in an exclusive and opposite sense when the term "Heaven" is invoked. It is true that some individual instances of Hildegard's terminology could be interpreted conventionally. Yet the following examples show both the inadequacy of taking them literally and the advantage of setting the conventional understandings in metaphoric tension with each other. The result of the tension between Heaven understood as afterlife and Heaven understood as present is an unexpected voice of authority that casts surprisingly new light on a perennial conundrum of human life.

Hildegard makes coherent these two types of meaning by structuring *Scivias* as a series of twenty-six visions, each followed by a detailed interpretation. In the visions she often adopts conventional uses of the term "Heaven." "Paradise," for example, in Vision One refers to the narrative setting of the Genesis myth, into which Adam and Eve were born and from which they were subsequently exiled. God, however, is not "in Heaven" either at the beginning or at the source of the vision: instead there is a figure on a mountain – "the One who is enthroned upon the mountain" (68) who dramatically gets the attention of human beings. At times this figure coincides with the expected location of Heaven – "Heaven was suddenly opened and a fiery and inestimable brilliance descended over that offering [of the Mass]" (237). Yet that expectation is cut short by the immediate introduction of ambiguity: "... the brilliance bore

it on high into the secret places of Heaven and then replaced it on the altar, as a person draws in a breath and lets it out again . . ." (237). For their
part, human beings are mediocre beings in the scale of created objects
who become something more than they are by nature. They both are and
are not divine.

Hildegard brought a fresh understanding to the then familiar analogical understanding of Heaven in relation to what was known through
earthly experience. Let us now see how her scientific understanding of
the cosmos supported, enhanced, and informed the roots of her religious
understanding.

Heaven in Cosmology: The Analogical

The second context for studying Hildegard's notion of Heaven is her cosmology. To gain entry to her cosmology, we reconstruct some part of the
world of ideas regarding the notion of Heaven as it existed six centuries
before the fatal split between science and religion that took place in the
seventeenth and eighteenth centuries, a split that resulted in two distinct
fields of interpretation – scientific cosmology and religious cosmology. By
Hildegard's time, the Ptolemaic theory of the universe, originating in
Alexandria in the second century C.E., had prevailed for nine hundred
years and would last yet another five hundred. Today, the superiority of
the sixteenth-century Copernican system over the Ptolemaic system
tends to obscure the relative adequacy that the Ptolemaic system enjoyed
for over fourteen hundred years. Many people today think 1) that Copernicus was the first to put the Sun, and not Earth, in the center of the universe; and 2) that the diminishment of the importance of the human
species was a necessary result of this displacement of Earth from the center.[23] However, in his *Cosmology*, Jean Charon reminds us that long before
Copernicus, the Greek astronomer Aristarchus of Samos (fl. ca. 20 B.C.E.)
proposed that Earth moves in a circle around a motionless Sun.[24] As far
as we know, the Greeks, and for that matter everyone else until Kepler in
the sixteenth century, used only circles and spheres in their cosmologies,
affirming Pythagoras's axiom that the sphere was the most perfect form
and taking it for granted, therefore, that it was the form of a theoretically
perfect universe. Greek arguments against Aristarchus's sun-centered or
heliocentric theory are not known. But six centuries after Aristarchus,

Ptolemy solved several of the questions the ancient Greeks had regarding the retrograde motion of the planets and, using epicycles – that is, circles attached to circles – accounted for their movements better than ever before.

Hildegard, using multiple wheels rotating both independently and as part of a universal system, incorporates some aspects of the Ptolemaic universe in her cosmology. In a chapter on Hildegard in his *History of Magic and Experimental Science during the First Thirteen Centuries of Our Era*, Lynn Thorndike wrote that Hildegard does more than merely apply conventional understandings of natural science to her religious perspective:

> A notable thing about even her religious visions is the essential conformity of their cosmology and physiology to the then prevalent theories of natural science. The theory of four elements, the hypothesis of concentric spheres surrounding the Earth, the current notions concerning veins and humors, are introduced with slight variations in visions supposed to be of divine origin. In matters of detail Hildegard may make mistakes, or at least differ from the then more generally accepted view and she displays no little originality in giving a new turn to some of the familiar concepts, as in her five powers of fire, four of air, fifteen of water, and seven of Earth. . . .

Thorndike concludes that "Hildegard certainly says that she sees the natural facts in her visions. The hypotheses of . . . natural science . . . are embodied in [her] reveries and utilized in inspired revelation. Science serves religion it is true, but religion for its part does not hesitate to accept science. . . ."[25] We should not be surprised, either, to find religious interest in her two works of medicine and natural history.

We find multiple uses of the term "Heaven" in Hildegard's cosmological reflections. One of the most common is her assertion that Heaven penetrates Earth with its winds that are the breath of the Spirit. From her *Causes and Cures*, consider the following analogies for understanding this mysterious relationship:

> The firmament comprises fire, sun, moon, stars, and winds. It exists through all of them and is firmed by their properties so that it

may not fall apart. As the soul holds the entire body of a human being, so the winds hold together the entire firmament to prevent its
destruction. These winds are invisible, just as the soul stemming
from God's secret place [one of Hildegard's code words for Heaven
in *Scivias*], is invisible. (26)

Later, in the same text, Heaven is a transformative agent working as the
Holy Spirit:

> The Holy spirit pervades the humans' entire nature. . . . This is
> made evident in the prophets, the wise, the good, and the just. And,
> in choosing everything good, the Holy Spirit, drawing them toward
> himself, permeates and illumines them as the sun permeates and il-
> lumines storms, so that this profusion of the fiery Holy spirit con-
> quers the humans' mutable nature, as is written, "Whatever is born
> of God conquers the world" [1 John 5:4]. And then humans do not
> sin. As cheap food is changed by the taste of spices into better tast-
> ing food, losing its poor taste, so by the fire of the Holy Spirit the
> humans' cheap nature is changed into a better nature than their
> conception implies. And thus human beings become different in na-
> ture because what is Heavenly conquers and overcomes what is
> Earthly. Therefore everything rejoices in God. . . . (34)

What is Heavenly "will out," in other words. That is reason for rejoicing.

Unlike the Augustinian Neoplatonic expectation of escape from the
body, Hildegard has a keen sense of how body and soul are intrinsically
bound to each other: the integration of the two constitutes the linchpin
between Heaven and Earth:

> The soul goes about in Earthly affairs, laboring through many
> changes as fleshly behavior demands. But the spirit raises itself in
> two ways: sighing, groaning and desiring God; and choosing among
> options in various matters as if by some rule, for the soul has dis-
> cernment in reason. Hence Man contains in himself the likeness of
> Heaven and Earth. In what way? He has a circle, which contains his
> clarity, breath and reason, as the sky has its lights, air and birds; and
> he has a receptacle containing humidity, germination and birth, as

the Earth contains fertility, fruition and animals. What is this? O human, you are wholly in every creature. . . . (*Scivias*, 151)

From a religious perspective, scientific understanding is woven into the theological.

Hildegard's reputation in the history of science is based primarily on her work in the *Physica* (a book of philosophy of the natural world) and in *Causes and Cures* (a description of the human being as a miniature of the universe, with an account of disorders affecting human beings).[26] Her contributions to science are noticed by early historians of science like Charles Singer,[27] who take observation to be the sine qua non of science. To be one of the few women of her time today credited with having contributed to experimental science is no small achievement. Nevertheless, her analogical vision of correspondences between the Heavenly cosmos and human beings is equally, and perhaps more importantly, a theoretical contribution. The residue of this analogical vision crops up throughout her work in different garments – sometimes moral reflections, sometimes physiological and sexual, sometimes political; it culminates in her last book, *The Book of Divine Works*, ten visions emphasizing the achievement of balance and unity in the cosmic law.

To see the theoretical dimension of her cosmology, we might contrast it with Grand Unification Theory made popular by the well-known physicists Stephen Hawking and Steven Weinberg. What Hawking, Weinberg, and others want to do is to reduce all the physical theories into one grand equation for the universe.[28] But to a theologian's ear, their claims sound much larger: Hawking uses the expression "and then we shall know the mind of God."[29] Unlike Hawking's and Weinberg's relatively narrow focus on physical causation – a focus that effectively excludes all living things – Hildegard's horizon includes all that exists, including the past, present, and future of *humankind*. Whereas Weinberg thinks that the "point" of the universe is that there is no point, Hildegard attempts to describe the "point" of the universe by making visible and audible the complex, ongoing, multifarious construction of the universe, emphasizing the distinctive and multicapacitied features of all that we call "human." Hildegard would not likely truck with the contemporary appreciation for ambiguity on this issue. In her "Letter to Monks," for example, she wrote that monks and nuns were the "new planets" that appeared at the time of the Christian nativity.

With respect to theory, Hildegard thinks human beings *are* the point of the universe. But since, as human beings, we can see only from a determinate – a finite – point in the universe, statistically, we never "realize" the whole as a whole and are conscious therefore of being usually in a state of defect. Nevertheless, we do have the capacity to "see" the whole imaginatively, analogically, and sometimes metaphorically. These empirical facts – the limitations to our capacity to embody that vision fully and constantly, the resulting discrepancy between vision and realization, as well as our visions – are all elements of Hildegard's work.

Hildegard had no illusions about the struggle involved in achieving this grand cosmology that was informed by both religious and scientific insight. In *Scivias*, for example, we also find the startling claim about the relationship between theological reflection and the presence of God on Earth:

> For people have within themselves struggles of confession and of denial. How? Because this one confesses Me, and that one denies Me. And in this struggle the question is: Is there a God or not? And the answer comes from the Holy Spirit Who dwells in the person: God is, and created you, and redeemed you. But as long as this question and answer are in a person, the power of God will not be absent from him, for this question and answer carries with it penitence. But when this question is not in a person, neither is the answer of the Holy Spirit, for such a person drives out God's gift from himself and, without the question that leads to penitence, throws himself upon death. And the Virtues display to God the battles of these wars, for they are the seal that shows God the intention that worships or denies Him. (*Scivias* 141)

In this passage we hear Hildegard's initial formulation of the *question* of God according to the theistic model we are familiar with since Anselm's formulation in the twelfth century: Does God exist? And because the empirical sciences have become normative for what human beings in our culture affirm as reality, the question is likely to be seen as being about some kind of external objective reality – a being findable only within the realm of religion, a being by definition excluded from the sciences. In Hildegard's time, however, the question "Does God exist?" was a larger metaphysical issue in the sense that the key word to be questioned is not

"God," but "exist." The answer was expected to state *the sense in which it was appropriate* to speak of God as "existing" or not. Unlike either Anselm or Thomas Aquinas, Hildegard does not use the newly found Aristotelian logic to respond. Instead, she sidesteps the issue of logic by stating that the answer will come from within the experience of the question: "But as long as this question and answer are in a person, the power of God will not be absent from him, for this question and answer carries with it penitence." There she locates what for her is the sine qua non of doing theological reflection.

Clearly, Hildegard did not succumb to an extrinsicist position even on what was to become the central theological question of the next nine centuries, and so we are now prepared to retrieve her understanding of Heaven in the context of her cosmology. But first we must make explicit that our way of thinking may resist such retrieval because there seems to be no place for the term "Heaven" in today's world of credible ideas. As Rudolf Bultmann wrote in his famous essay, "On the Problem of Demythologizing": ". . . Myth talks about this transcendent reality and power inadequately when it represents the transcendent as spatially distant, as Heaven above the Earth or as hell beneath it."[30] It is clear from the remainder of his essay that Bultmann was not recommending that we kill the myths or eliminate cultic concepts, but that we interpret them. But the three-story universe has been rejected in favor of the Copernican and the Einsteinian, and the scientific world of meanings has acquired an unquestioned matter-of-fact intelligibility even when these meanings are hardly understood or not understood at all. By contrast, serious theological reflection has lost its matter-of-fact intelligibility and, as a result, the very term "Heaven" has been heavily discredited in theological as well as scientific circles. The need to demythologize – that is, to distinguish theological meaning from objectified meaning – resulted instead in demythicizing, in eliminating the elements rather than interpreting them.

Nevertheless, the medieval scientific cosmology survived the scientific universe and is still argued for in some quarters today. Because of its allegorical nature, classical cosmology seems much richer than what came after, when cosmology was made to conform to contemporary scientific cosmology. Hildegard's cosmology and the place of Heaven in it provide good examples of just how rich is its potential for analogy. Essentially, "Heaven" for Hildegard was an integral part of the universe. It would have been inconceivable to her to experience Heaven as being separate from the places she inhabited. This does not mean that she restricted the concept of Heaven to these places. It means only that "Heaven" was an aspect of the experience of transcendence in and through particular events and places.

Heaven in Liturgy: The Experiential

Our third context for studying Hildegard's notion of Heaven is in her approach to liturgy. There, her ability to see human beings in the "likeness of Heaven and Earth" is most keenly realized in her songs and rubrics for liturgical celebrations. The extent to which she took this likeness seriously can be seen first of all in an exchange of letters between Hildegard and the superior of the sisters at Andernach over "certain strange and irregular practices" in Hildegard's monastery:

> They say that on feast days your virgins stand in the church with unbound hair when singing the psalms and that as part of their dress they wear white, silk veils, so long that they touch the floor. Moreover, it is said that they wear crowns of gold filigree, into which are inserted crosses on both sides and the back, with a figure of the Lamb on the front, and that they adorn their fingers with golden rings. (Letter 52)

Hildegard responded with a defense of the liturgical practices in question. She also displays her view of Heaven with her explanation of a virgin's life:

> . . . But these strictures [regarding clothing for a married woman] do not apply to a virgin, for she stands in the unsullied purity of paradise lovely and unwithering and she always remains in the full vitality of the budding rod. . . . Virgins are married with holiness in the Holy Spirit. . . . Thus . . . it is appropriate for a virgin to wear a white vestment, . . . considering that her mind is made one with the interwoven whole, and keeping in mind the One to whom she is joined as it is written, . . . "These follow the Lamb whithersoever he goeth" [Apoc. 1:4]. (Letter 52r)[31]

This defense is followed by a somewhat gratuitous (and cutting) reference to the need for ranks in Heaven: "It is clear that differentiation must be maintained in these matters, lest . . . the nobility of their character be torn asunder when they slaughter one another out of hatred." Hildegard concludes that God "establishes ranks on Earth, just as in Heaven with angels, archangels, [etc.]. And they are all loved by God, although they are not equal in rank" (ibid.). But her music conveys an even more credible sense of Heaven.

Listening to some of the more than seventy liturgical antiphons and propers from Barbara Newman's definitive collection *Saint Hildegard of Bingen Symphonia* – which she aptly subtitled "The Harmonious Music of Heavenly Mysteries" – one can believe without exaggeration that Hildegard came closest to experiencing Heaven in the liturgy. Newman shows that Hildegard used images like "building" to "evoke the Godward striving of the Earthborn" and that of "the City" to set each individual saint "in counterpoint with the full community of the redeemed" (49). The intimate connection of text and music[32] can be heard in pieces she composed for individual occasions as well as those she claims to have received during visions.

One of the loveliest, "O presul vere civitatis" (available in the Harmonia compact disc entitled *A Feather on the Breath of God*), conveys her sense of the relation between each saint's life of "spiritual effort on Earth and his or her glory in Heaven."[33] Hildegard composed this sequence (a hymn traditionally sung at Mass just before the Gospel) for the liturgical feast of the Irish monk who was founder of the hermitage that eventually became the monastery, St. Disibod. She wrote the music and lyrics at the request of the abbot a few years after she had left with her nuns to found the Rupertsberg.

> O dance-leader of the true city,
> who in the temple with the finial-stone
> soaring Heavenwards
> was prostrate on the Earth
> for God.
> You, wanderer of the seed of Man,
> longed to be an exile
> for the love of Christ.

O summit of the cloistered mind
you tirelessly showed a beautiful face
in the mirror of the dove.

You lived hidden in a secluded place,
intoxicated with the aroma of flowers,
reaching forth to God
through the lattices of the saints.

O gable on the cloisters of Heaven,
because you have bartered the world
for an unclouded life
you will always have this prize,
o nourishing witness.

For in your mind
the living fountain in clearest light
courses purest rills
through the channel of salvation.

You are an immense tower
before the altar of the Highest
and you cloud the roof of this tower
with the smoke of perfumes.

O Disibod, by your light,
and with models of pure sound,
you have wondrously built aisles of praise
with two parts
through the Son of Man.

You stand on high
not blushing before the living God,
and you cover all with refreshing dew:
let us praise God with these words:

O sweet life,
and O blessed constancy,
within the celestial Jerusalem
has always built a glorious light
in this blessed Disibod.

Now praise be to God
in the worthy form
of the meaningful, beautiful tonsure.

And let the Heavenly citizens
rejoice in those
who have imitated them in this way.

One would like to leave Hildegard here – in apparent ecstasy. Doing so, however, would hide her own distinctive way of Earth-dwelling – a way that was only secondarily contemplative and that went a longer distance in service to others and in pursuit of justice. Paul Kaiser, for example, thought that "her medical skill contributed more to her popular reputation for saintliness than all her writings,"[34] and Sabina Flanagan points out that the third part of the earliest biography allots disproportionate attention to Hildegard's cure of a woman no one else could help.

Even more revealing of her priorities is the story of her resisting church authorities on the issue of her burial of a nobleman in consecrated ground. Hildegard had ministered to the man, who had previously been excommunicated, and was convinced of his reconciliation with God. When the authorities proscribed the celebration of liturgy at their convent, one can imagine the pain of Hildegard and the nuns at being deprived of the ritual that was at the heart of their monastic lives. The dispute was settled months after Hildegard wrote a fiery letter – equivalent to a "theology of music" – to the church authorities on the importance of sacred song.[35]

Can we not conclude that, for Hildegard, Heaven is strictly speaking both *here* and *there*, *then* and *now*? Heaven is a place where justice and healing come to be. It is utopian in the sense of a time and place yet to come, but also a capability of the already here and now. And it can be perceived at any site and at any moment – most acutely in special moments, such as in visions and in liturgies – wherever and whenever ordinary experience becomes holy and the human becomes divine.

NOTES

1. See J. G. Davies, *Daily Life of Early Christians* (New York: Duell Sloan and Pearce, 1953), xi–xii.

2. See Chris Hellier, *Monasteries of Greece* (London: Tauris Parke Books; New York: St. Martin's Press, 1996); and Sacheverrell Sitwell, *Monks, Nuns, and Monasteries* (New York: Holt Rinehart and Winston, 1985).

3. The other two are the mystical writings of Elizabeth of Schonau and the illustrated encyclopedia *Hortus deliciarum* (Garden of Delights) of Herrad of Landsberg.

4. Barbara Newman, introduction, translations, and commentary, *Saint Hildegard of Bingen Symphonia: A Critical Edition of the* Symphonia armonie celestium revelationum [Symphony of the Harmony of Celestial Revelations] (Ithaca, N.Y., and London: Cornell University Press, 1988), xi.

5. The private language consists of *Lingua ignota*, a word list for a secret language, and *Litterae ignotae*, a secret writing system, both written between 1151 and 1158.

6. Sabina Flanagan, *Hildegard of Bingen, 1098–1179: A Visionary Life*, 2d ed. (New York and London: Routledge, 1998).

7. See Hildegard of Bingen, *The Book of the Rewards of Life (Liber Vitae Meritorum)*, trans. Bruce W. Hozeski (New York and Oxford: Oxford University Press, 1994).

8. In her preface to *The Book of the Rewards of Life*, however, Hildegard seems to include her scientific writings in the visionary mode: "This was the first year after that vision had shown me the *simplicity of the various natural creatures* with responses and warnings for greater and lesser people" (p. 9).

9. See Charles Singer, *From Magic to Science: Essays on the Scientific Twilight* (New York: Dover Publications, 1958). Singer, who later became a historian of science, rather smugly assumes that her cause for canonization was turned down: "Those who have impartially traced her life in her documents will, we believe, agree with the verdict of the church. . . ." Although "hers was a fiery, a prophetic, in many ways a singularly noble spirit, . . . she exhibited defects of character which prevent us from regarding her as a woman of truly saintly mind or life" (p. 203).

10. Flanagan, *Hildegard of Bingen*, 13.

11. Hildegard of Bingen, *On Natural Philosophy and Medicine, Selections from Cause et Curae*, trans. and intro. by Margret Berger (Cambridge: D. S. Brewer, 1999), 4.

12. Singer, *From Magic to Science*, viii, 232, and 238. Even though his essay "The Visions of Hildegard of Bingen," in *From Magic to Science*, 199–239, was published thirty-seven years after his two-volume study of the history of science (see note 27 below), it was written before the latter – while Singer was a pathologist and be-

fore his work in the history of science. Apart from his materialistic explanation of the basis of her visions and dismissal of the value of her scientific work, Singer provides an interesting descriptive account of her visions and cosmology.

13. See, for example, Paul Ricoeur, *Interpretation Theory: Discourse and the Surplus of Meaning* (Fort Worth: Texas Christian University Press, 1976): ". . . what is 'made one's own' is not something mental, not the intention of another subject, hidden behind the text, but the project of a world, the pro-position of a mode of being in the world that the text opens up in front of itself by means of its non-ostensive references" (p. 94).

14. I have used the following editions for all quotations from the five texts: Hildegard of Bingen, *Scivias*, trans. Mother Columba Hart and Jane Bishop (New York: Paulist Press, 1990); *Causes and Cures*, in Hildegard of Bingen, *On Natural Philosophy and Medicine, Selections from* Cause et Curae, trans. and intro. by Margret Berger (Cambridge: D. S. Brewer, 1999); Hildegard of Bingen, *The Book of the Rewards of Life (Liber Vitae Meritorum)*, trans. Bruce W. Hozeski (New York and Oxford: Oxford University Press, 1994); *The Book of Divine Works: Ten Visions of God's Deeds in the World and Humanity*, trans. Robert Cunningham, from Heinrich Schipperges's German translation (*Welt und Mensch: Das Buch "De operatione Dei"* [Salzburg: Otto Müller Verlag, 1965]) of Hildegard's medieval Latin text, in *Hildegard of Bingen's Book of Divine Works with Letters and Songs*, ed. and intro. Matthew Fox (Santa Fe, N.M.: Bear and Company, 1987); Barbara Newman, introduction, translations, and commentary, *Saint Hildegard of Bingen Symphonia: A Critical Edition of the* Symphonia aramonie celestium revelationum [Symphony of the Harmony of Celestial Revelations] (Ithaca, N.Y., and London: Cornell University Press, 1988).

15. In some depictions of her visions, thought to have been painted by a contemporary, however, her scribe is shown writing as she receives the vision.

16. Hildegard of Bingen, *Scivias*, trans. Hart and Bishop, 25.

17. Marymay Downing, "Prehistoric Goddesses: The Cretan Challenge," *Journal of Feminist Studies in Religion* 1 (spring 1985): 7–22.

18. I knew the names of both foundations from collections of women's writings – Bingen being part of the now famous Hildegard's identity; and Helfta (in the former East Germany), the thirteenth-century religious house of the two Gertrudes (Gertrude the Great and Gertrude of Hackeborn) and the two Mechthilds (Mechthild of Magdeburg and Mechthild of Hackeborn).

19. The painting is the center panel of the Isenheim Altarpiece in the Unterlinden Museum in Colmar, Germany. See Heinrich Schipperges, *The World of Hildegard of Bingen: Her Life, Times, and Visions* (Collegeville, Minn.: The Liturgical Press, 1998), 42–43; translated by John Cumming from the original German *Die Welt von Hildegard von Bingen* (Freiburg im Breisgau: Verlag Herder, 1997).

20. Recent recordings include *"Sequentia" Ordo Virtutum* (Deutsche Harmonia Mundi 05472-77394-2 [2 CDs]; *11,000 Virgins* (Harmonia Mundi 907200 France); *Monk and the Abbess* (BMG Catalyst 09026-68329-2); *Laudes de Ste. Ursula* (Harmonia Mundi 901616 France); and *Early Music* (Nonesuch 79457; includes "O Virtus sapientiae" by John Cage).

21. Because of Hildegard's extraordinary practice of recording her age and often the year at the beginning of each text, readers can correlate where she was living at the time each text was written.

22. For this theory of metaphor, see Mary Gerhart and Allan M. Russell, *New Maps for Old: Explorations in Science and Religion* (New York and London: Continuum, 2001), 7–78.

23. See Dennis R. Danielson, "The Great Copernican Cliché," *American Journal of Physics* 69 (October 2001): 1029–35.

24. See Jean E. Charon, *Cosmology*, trans. Patrick Moore (New York: McGraw Hill, 1970), 34–37.

25. Lynn Thorndike, *History of Magic and Experimental Science during the First Thirteen Centuries of Our Era* (New York: Macmillan, 1923–58), 131–32, 134.

26. For the complicated manuscript tradition of both *Causes and Cures* and *Physica* (which originally may have been two parts of a single text entitled *Liber subtilitatum diuersarum naturarum creaturarum* [Book of the Intricacies of the Diverse Natures of Creatures]), see Hildegard of Bingen, *On Natural Philosophy and Medicine*, trans. Berger, ix–xi.

27. In the history of science, the major dissenting voice regarding the importance of Hildegard's work is Charles Singer's essay, "Greek Biology and Its Relation to the Rise of Modern Biology," in his *Studies in the History and Method of Science* (Oxford: Clarendon Press, 1917–21). Writing before the early twentieth-century retrieval of texts from the Middle Ages, Singer declared that "during the Dark Ages, and even until the twelfth or thirteenth century, there were no effective additions to botanical knowledge." In Singer's view, aside from the reproduction of three earlier Latin texts, the study of plants was in a "long depression" that lasted until Albertus Magnus's *De Vegetabilibus plantis*: even this "essentially learned product," based on a first century B.C.E. text, is "marred [by the scholastic doctrine that] philosophia is concerned with generalities, not particulars" – a doctrine taken to explain "the failure of scholasticism to erect an enduring scientific structure." In Singer's version of the Middle Ages, Hildegard is not worthy of mention except as the wrongly attributed author of a thirteenth-century text. Singer also perpetuates the myth of the separation of science and religion by claiming that "the extensive literature that has risen around the life and works of Hildegard has come from the hands of writers who have shown no interest in natural knowledge" (73–74). But most other early commentators are critically ap-

preciative of Hildegard's accomplishments. According to Lynn Thorndike, Singer (in his research on Hildegard in German universities) ignores the work of Paul Kaiser, *Die Naturwissenschaftliche Schriften der Hl. Hildegard* (1901), and E. Wasmann, "Hildegard von Bingen als ältestedeutsche Naturforscherin" (1913). Noticing that Hildegard seems to be familiar with Bernard of Silvestris's *De Mundi Universitate*, Thorndike, in *A History of Magic and Experimental Science*, devotes a whole chapter to Hildegard's scientific work, as does George Sarton, who regards Hildegard as "the most original medical writer of Latindom in the twelfth century." In his multivolume *History of Science* (Baltimore: Carnegie Institution of Washington, 1931), Sarton writes: "Her medical knowledge can be traced back to Roman sources through the unbroken Benedictine tradition; she also knew the popular remedies – mostly herbs – of her people. . . . She names about a thousand plants and animals in the German vernacular" (70, 386–88).

28. Some scientists think that Hawking and Weinberg have developed a way of something seemingly grand and large for the purpose of attracting attention to science and to show that science is capable of dealing with the larger questions. For a contemporary theological formulation of the larger "limit-questions," see David Tracy, *Plurality and Ambiguity: Hermeneutics, Religion, Hope* (San Francisco: Harper and Row, 1987), e.g., "the questions provoked by the sense that in every act of resistance some strange and unnameable hope, however inchoate, betrays itself" (86–87).

29. Stephen Hawking speaks of the ambition of science as "knowing the mind of God" in the video recording *Mastering the Universe* (Chicago: Capital Cities/ABC Video Enterprises, Inc., 1985).

30. In Rudolf Bultmann, *New Testament and Mythology and Other Basic Writings*, ed. and trans. Schubert Ogden (Philadelphia: Fortress Press, 1984), 98.

31. Both letters are included in *The Letters of Hildegard of Bingen*, trans. Joseph L. Baird and Radd K. Ehrman, vol. 1 (New York and Oxford: Oxford University Press), 127–30.

32. Newman, *Saint Hildegard of Bingen Symphonia*, 49, thinks that their "mutual enrichment" has hardly been addressed.

33. Ibid.

34. See Thorndike, *A History of Magic and Experimental Science*, 125, n. 1.

35. Schipperges, *The World of Hildegard of Bingen*, 62.

MYTHS OF THE UNDERWORLD IN CONTEMPORARY AMERICAN MILLENNIALISM

MICHAEL BARKUN

"Place" is as much a product of mind as of space. Indeed, as utopian writers have demonstrated for centuries, a nonexistent place sometimes exercises greater attraction than one that can actually be visited. The imagined places of utopian fiction do not, however, exhaust the realm of nonexistent worlds. The worlds I describe here are of this sort – places that are far from utopian (indeed, they often have dystopian attributes), but exist solely in the minds of believers. At the same time, unlike the constructed places of fiction, these are asserted actually to exist, notwithstanding massive evidence to the contrary.

Beliefs about these places flourish in contemporary American subcultures. Some of these are built around fundamentalist religion, some around extreme right-wing politics, and some around occult and esoteric teachings. They are, however, linked by a common disposition to see the world in conspiracist terms, controlled by hidden, malevolent powers. Just as these secret rulers allegedly control politics and the economy, so they are believed to have suppressed knowledge about hidden worlds.

These conspiracy theories are generally built around the concept of a coming "New World Order," understood to be the reign of the ultimate forces of evil in the world which will, in the end-times, do battle with the

forces of good. In its religious variant, the New World Order is synony-
mous with the rule of Antichrist during the pre-Armageddon Tribulation.
Secular apocalypticists see the New World Order as the vehicle of evil
elites operating through such organizations as the Illuminati and the Tri-
lateral Commission. Whether religious or secular, New World Order
theories contain much the same paraphernalia of domination and
control – black helicopters, implanted microchips, and UN occupation
forces.

Beginning about 1990, these ideas began to surface in a quite different
milieu, one that was neither conventionally religious nor politically radi-
cal. That milieu was the subculture of believers in UFOs. Within a few
years, the UFO subculture began to manifest the full range of New World
Order ideas, linked now to the alleged presence on earth of alien beings.
How that migration of ideas took place is a subject for another day, and I
ask that you accept that it has in fact occurred. In the course of mapping
this diffusion among "ufologists," as they often call themselves, I found a
strange doctrinal mutation. This mutation identifies the New World Order tyranny with a nonhuman race at times called the "Serpent Race" or
the "Serpent People," and sometimes "reptilians" or "reptoids." It places
the center of power of this race not in outer space, but literally in the underworld, in subterranean caverns, passages, and tunnels that allegedly
lie deep within the earth. This race will in time, they believe, fight an ultimate battle with human beings.

Where, I wondered, had such ideas come from? They certainly were
not part of earlier New World Order conceptions, whether in the religious
form given them by Texe Marrs, Pat Robertson, and other evangelists; or
in the secular conceptions developed by the John Birch Society, militias,
and other antigovernment groups. Nor do they seem to have been part of
"ufology" before the late 1980s.

Much of this material resembles what folklorists call "urban legends" –
those widely diffused tales that the teller assures listeners are true, but
that always come indirectly from "a friend of a friend." In this case, however, much of the diffusion occurred widely and rapidly through the Internet, and much of the process of development can be traced. I am rea-
sonably confident that I have established the sources and lines of
transmission. While some of the connections remain conjectural, what I

am about to present seems the most likely scenario. I want first to describe it, and then to briefly discuss its implications for an understanding of contemporary millennialism.

I

On December 1, 1987, in Las Vegas, Nevada, a lengthy press statement was released by John Lear. Lear was an airline pilot previously employed by the CIA and the son of the inventor William P. Lear. John Lear's statement included, among other bizarre claims, assertions that extraterrestrials were regular visitors to the earth; that the United States government had entered into a treaty with them; and that this treaty exchanged alien technology for the right to abduct and study American citizens. In furtherance of this supposed agreement, Lear said, a number of underground laboratories had been built, operated jointly by the aliens and the CIA, most notably a vast underground facility supposedly constructed near Dulce, New Mexico, where unspeakable experiments were going on, and where combat had allegedly broken out between ourselves and the aliens.[1] Three points need to be made about Lear's statement: First, the aliens were described as unimaginably malevolent and devious; they were not spiritually advanced "space brothers." Second, the evil and violence were fundamentally located underground; and third, Lear made no mention of serpent creatures or reptilians.

That omission was quickly repaired. By 1989, the Lear story had been modified, identifying the aliens as a "Reptilian Humanoid Species" which could crossbreed with human beings,[2] and had transformative powers, allowing them to change shape and appear to be human when required.[3] There was disagreement about whether the reptilians had always lived underground; whether they had once lived on earth, only to leave it and return; or whether they originated in some distant star system. There was no disagreement, however, about their capacity for evil, their hostility to the human race, or the fact that they were now ensconced in subterranean warrens from which they could not be readily dislodged.

Although this "inner earth" material appeared in print, it proliferated initially on the Internet, where entire web sites have been devoted to its elaboration.[4] By 1999, the Internet literature began to spread in print, notably through the widely circulated work of the British New Age writer David Icke.[5]

It is easy to describe what might be called the "reptilian scenario," but much more difficult to pin down its origins. It was in fact the result of three separate but convergent influences: pseudoscientific "hollow earth" theories, theosophy and its offshoots, and pulp fiction published between the 1920s and the 1940s.

I shall say relatively little about hollow earth theories, beyond observing that despite overwhelming evidence to the contrary, they have been held by small coteries of believers in the nineteenth and twentieth centuries.[6] With the exception of a few variants that place us on the inner surface of a sphere, most hollow earth writers claim that another reality, allegedly with its own inhabitants and civilizations, exists somewhere beneath our feet, a fact which, in their view, scientists have either ignored or suppressed. Virtually all of the believers in reptilians subscribe to some version of the hollow earth model.

Theosophical influences require more attention, if only because they have commanded a far larger audience. In fact, H. P. Blavatsky, while not a hollow earth believer, was profoundly interested in an underground world. Under the influence of the nineteenth-century Atlantis writer and Populist politician Ignatius Donnelly, Madame Blavatsky accepted the notion that a superior civilization had once existed on Atlantis, before the latter disappeared in a prehistoric catastrophe. She concluded that while the continent had vanished, many of its works had not, particularly a worldwide "net-work [sic] of subterranean passages running in all directions."[7]

The linkage of lost continents and secret tunnels had an evident appeal to the latter-day theosophist Guy W. Ballard. Ballard claimed that in 1930, while truth-seeking on the slopes of Mt. Shasta, he met the Ascended Master, St. Germain, who whisked him to caverns beneath the Grand Teton Mountains.[8] Mt. Shasta had long been linked to lost continents in the minds of occultists, so that it was scarcely surprising that others claimed to have experienced epiphanies on its slopes. Ballard, founder of the I AM movement, was clearly the most prominent of these seekers, but more important for our purposes was an obscure occultist, Claude Doggins, aka Maurice Doreal.

In about 1930, "Dr. Doreal," as he preferred to be known, founded the

Brotherhood of the White Temple in Denver. Sometime later – probably in the late 1940s – the Brotherhood relocated to a valley west of Sedalia, Colorado, the better to survive a nuclear war, which Doreal predicted would occur in 1953.[9] He claimed that in 1931, the year after Ballard's epiphany, two Atlanteans waylaid him after a Los Angeles lecture and transported him to a gigantic cavern twelve miles beneath Mt. Shasta.[10] The details of Doreal's visit need not detain us. More to the point, in subsequent years, as he developed an "inner earth" cosmology, he began to describe races that supposedly inhabited the underground regions, information he received from the Atlanteans. Under the Brotherhood of the White Temple's auspices, Doreal issued nearly one hundred pamphlets on a wide range of occult and spiritual topics. Two are of particular relevance here.

In a pamphlet called "Mysteries of the Gobi," Doreal offered an exotic revisionist history of the world, one of whose key features was an ancient war between human beings and a "Serpent Race." The latter, he wrote, had "bodies like man, but . . . heads . . . like a great snake and . . . bodies faintly scaled. . . ." They also possessed hypnotic powers that allowed them to appear fully human when necessary.[11] Doreal suggested that in this era of primeval warfare, the Serpent Race had been exterminated. However, in another, and possibly later, publication – "Flying Saucers: An Occult Viewpoint" – Doreal significantly altered his position, arguing now that the Serpent Race were extraterrestrials and had not been destroyed. Instead, its members existed in a state of suspended animation, to be revived in the twentieth century as allies of Antichrist.[12] Many of the same ideas also appear in a long poem, "The Emerald Tablets," which Doreal professed to have translated from an original by "Thoth the Atlantean." Thoth/Doreal warned: "Yet, beware, the serpent still liveth / in a place that is open at times to the world. / Unseen they walk among thee."[13]

Where did Doreal's ideas come from? To be sure, he claimed to be privy to secret ancient knowledge, but for those of a more skeptical turn of mind, that scarcely suffices. The issue is made more complex by the fact that it is difficult to date his writings. He apparently began to publish about 1940 and continued to do so until his death in 1963.[14] His work from the early 1940s consists of fairly traditional biblical exegesis. Most of the pamphlets, if they bear any date at all, bear those of their most recent reprintings. It seems likely, however, that the material on the Serpent Race first appeared sometime between the mid-1940s and the failed nuclear war prediction in 1953.

That still leaves open the question of sources, an issue whose resolution requires us to move to an altogether different genre, the realm of pulp fiction.

II

In all likelihood, the notion of a shape-changing serpent race first came from the imagination of an obscure pulp fiction author, Robert E. Howard. Howard was a fantasy writer of the sword-and-sorcery variety, whose best-known creation was Conan the Barbarian – a dubious distinction, to be sure. In August 1929, Howard published a story in *Weird Tales* called "The Shadow Kingdom," in which the evil power was the snake-men. These creatures had the bodies of men but the heads of serpents. They also had the capacity to change shape, appearing human when they wished. Thought to have been destroyed, they returned, insinuating themselves into positions of power.[15]

While the first and fullest description of these creatures appears in Howard's work, he shared a common mythology with two other *Weird Tales* authors, Clarke Ashton Smith and the much better known H. P. Lovecraft. Both Ashton Smith and Lovecraft incorporated serpent men into their own work.[16]

Is there any reason to believe that Doreal and other occultists knew about and appropriated such material? While there is no direct evidence, there is some compelling circumstantial evidence. To appreciate it, we must turn once more to the "inner earth."

In 1945, another pulp magazine, *Amazing Stories*, began to publish the work of a hitherto unknown author, Richard Shaver. His work (or at least work attributed to him) appeared in three-fourths of the magazine's issues between 1945 and 1948. Shaver had written to the *Amazing Stories* editor, Raymond Palmer, claiming that he heard voices emanating from unknown subterranean civilizations. Shaver seems clearly to have been delusional. He first heard voices through his welding equipment at a Ford Motor Company plant. Initially, he heard the thoughts of fellow workers, but they were soon displaced by voices he came to believe originated in the "inner earth." In time, he found that he could hear the voices even without his welding equipment and began to write accounts of their world.[17]

Shaver's first extensive publication – a novelet called "I Remember Lemuria!" – evoked the lost continent of Lemuria (also called Mu) and, like most of Shaver's work, had been extensively rewritten to incorporate the conventions of pulp fiction. Raymond Palmer, who did much of the doctoring, tried to get Shaver to adopt the style of Edgar Rice Burroughs, with little success. But despite the presence of characters, dialogue, and plot, in the manner of *Amazing Stories'* other authors, the magazine presented the Shaver stories as true, lightly retouched to make them more entertaining. Sensing a circulation-builder, Palmer dubbed them "the Shaver Mystery," a label which continues to stick to the material.[18]

At the core of "the Shaver Mystery" was the contention that a deadly struggle was going on deep underground between two "inner earth" species, one good and one evil, with the strong likelihood that we surface dwellers would become involved. The stories stimulated a large number of readers' letters, many of which were published. In August 1946, the editors wrote a short piece recommending Maurice Doreal's pamphlets to "all students of the Shaver matter." Doreal himself responded with a letter the following month, confirming that there was indeed evil afoot in underground caverns, and that humanity might well be a target.[19] However, neither the article about Doreal nor his own letter mentioned the "Serpent Race." One of the pamphlets dealing with the "Serpent Race" – "Flying Saucers: An Occult View" – had almost certainly not yet been published, since the term "flying saucers" did not come into use until the following year. What is certain is that the editors of *Amazing Stories* knew about Doreal, and he, in turn, knew about them and about "the Shaver Mystery."

A similar exchange took place in 1947, this time when the editors reported that a certain W. C. Hefferlin had written a letter asserting that "flying saucers" came from a place called "Rainbow City," a city beneath the South Pole. A letter from Hefferlin to that effect was published in January 1948, although it may not have been the one initially referred to.[20] At the time, Hefferlin and his wife were privately circulating a manuscript about flying saucers and underground cities in Antarctica, extending a continuing interest in polar matters by hollow earth believers.[21] The essence of "the Hefferlin manuscript" was subsequently published in a 1960 pamphlet directed at New Age readers.[22]

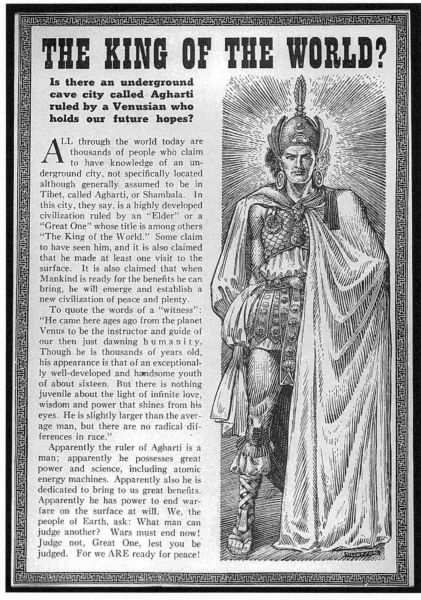

Fig. 1. This illustration of the messianic monarch of a subterranean Tibetan kingdom appeared in the May 1946 issue of *Amazing Stories*, a pulp science-fiction magazine, whose editor, Raymond Palmer, was instrumental in popularizing ideas about underground civilizations. (George Arents Research Library, Syracuse University)

At the same time that the Shaver material was appearing, *Amazing Stories* also began to feature articles and stories about "Agharti," supposedly an underground city beneath Tibet or some adjacent part of Inner Asia. This legend seems to have developed first in French literature around the turn of the twentieth century,[23] but the principle conduit in English was a 1922 volume by the prolific Polish scientist and adventurer Ferdinand Ossendowski.[24]

Ossendowski devoted his final four chapters to an account of stories he claimed to have heard from Mongol and Tibetan guides, princes, and lamas. According to these tales, Agharti and subsidiary underground realms were ruled by the "King of the World," a spiritually advanced figure of messianic proportions, who at some future time would "lead all the good people of the world against all the bad. . . ." At the end of history, this subterranean monarch would lead his people to the surface to effect the final millennial consummation.[25]

This was enough to start *Amazing Stories* editor Raymond Palmer on one of his customary riffs, and in May 1946, he himself wrote a short but prominently displayed piece called "The King of the World?" In Palmer's hands, Agharti's ruler became a Venusian who would, "when Mankind is ready, . . . emerge and establish a new civilization of peace and plenty."[26] A month later, one of Palmer's authors, Heinrich Hauser, summarized Ossendowski's account. The "King of the World" was one of a long line of elevated souls who, despite their remote location, used telepathy to influence "men of destiny" on the surface.[27]

While Shaver described an "inner earth" where the powers of evil might defeat the powers of good, the Agharti literature suggested that the outcome was not in doubt. The underground "King of the World" would prevail.

Thus, the worlds of pulp fiction authors, hollow earth believers, UFO enthusiasts, and occultists were interpenetrating in complex ways by the late 1940s and continued to do so in succeeding decades.

The final evidence that this was the case is supplied by a 1951 publication, Robert Ernst Dickhoff's *Agharta*.[28] Dickhoff claimed to be the Sungma Red Lama of the Dordjelutru Lamasery, an institution apparently headquartered in Dickhoff's New York City bookshop.[29] Although Dickhoff does not refer directly to any of the authors discussed here, he seems to have read them all. He cites "The Emerald Tablets" in passing, but neglects to mention Doreal.[30] Otherwise, with slight modifications, he puts most of the pieces together: The humanoid serpent men came from Venus. They exploited the antediluvian tunnel system to infiltrate and capture Atlantis and Lemuria, whose survivors escaped to such underground hideouts as Agharta (which he places beneath the Sangpo Valley in China) and Rainbow City in the Antarctic. The serpent men appear to have been defeated, but they and their agents have in reality infiltrated high policymaking circles through their powers of mind control. The remaining reptilians lie in subterranean polar suspended animation, awaiting the moment to strike.[31] In the late 1980s, John Lear and others would add UFOs and underground laboratories to complete the picture.

III

What are we to make of this strange conglomeration of occultism and fantasy? I want to address this question in two ways, first by indicating the explicit links with millennialism, and then by exploring the implications for the contemporary millenarian climate.

The linkages with millennialism are fairly explicit, revolving around the belief that a power of ultimate evil exists and that, although frustrated in the past, it remains sufficiently potent to make one final thrust for power. When it does so, the outcome of the battle will definitively determine who rules the cosmos. The distinctive feature of the struggle is that all or a significant part of it will occur underground, in a hidden realm of caverns, tunnels, and subterranean cities – a literal underworld. Much of this literature contains elaborate maps that purport to show the locations of tunnels, installations, and surface entry points. Earlier occultists, like Blavatsky, emphasized tunnels in South America, or underground cities in the Himalayas. Contemporary ufologists have added a new locus of concern in the American Southwest, pointing to such otherwise obscure places as Dulce, New Mexico.

The equating of snakes with evil has, of course, a special resonance in Western religion, a connection that has not escaped the creators of this literature. They are quick to point out that the story of the serpent in the Garden is evidence of a reptilian who walks upright and converses. Doreal and Dickhoff, among others, regarded the tale of the Fall as simply the best-known expression of the serpent race's malevolence.[32] In so doing, they connect to an older exegetical tradition that speculated about the serpent's humanoid qualities, such as its ability to engage Eve in a persuasive conversation. As I demonstrated in an earlier examination of the Christian Identity movement, contemporary white supremacists have also revisited this tradition in order to construct a satanic ancestry for the descendants of Cain.[33] In the hands of "inner earth" writers, the serpent in Genesis functions as merely the best-known member of a diabolical, primeval race whose arts of concealment and dissimulation are believed to continue to the present day as part of the struggle between God and Satan. Thus, claims of reptilian shape-shifting and mind control replace the biblical serpent's more conventional rhetorical talents.

If the underworld functions as the locus for primal evil, it carries a more ambiguous set of meanings as well, since it is also seen as a place of refuge into which the beleaguered forces of virtue can withdraw to fight another day. It appears in this guise as a sanctuary for the survivors of Atlantis and Lemuria, and therefore the repository of their ancient wisdom. It is also the locale of Agharta, from which spiritual masters seek to redeem life on the surface. In a few cases, such beliefs were linked to the literal construction of underground bomb shelters, so that the spiritually enlightened might save themselves from nuclear calamity. That was the reason Maurice Doreal took the Brotherhood of the White Temple from Denver to Sedalia, anticipating the better-known shelter program of the I AM offshoot, Elizabeth Clare Prophet's Montana-based Church Universal and Triumphant.[34]

These tales not only illuminate a strange strand in contemporary apocalyptic literature; they also exemplify major characteristics that distinguish contemporary millennialism. Let me conclude, then, by examining two such characteristics. The first is what I shall call "fact-fiction reversals." The second is a variety of millennialism I term the "improvisational style."

Certainly, one of the most striking characteristics of the current "inner earth" literature is its casual attitude toward the difference between fact and fiction. This is not unusual. An increasing range of apocalyptic literature treats "fact" and "fiction" as reversible categories, according to which what is ordinarily deemed "fact" may be dismissed as "fiction," and what purports to be "fiction" is really encoded "fact."

The conversion of "fact" into "fiction" occurs whenever received or mainstream knowledge claims are dismissed as distortions or fabrications. This is particularly common in conspiracy theories, with their assertion that the apparent holders of power are mere pawns in the hands of hidden conspirators. The same dismissal of conventional wisdom occurs in the elaborate arguments by "inner earth" and UFO writers that official positions, whether on the structure of the earth or the presence of extraterrestrials, are a façade of lies behind which the truth is concealed. Whatever comes from centers of power – governmental, religious, or academic – is regarded as suspect on its face.

By the same token, the credence given to the apparently fictional is just as striking. Raymond Palmer's decision to package Richard Shaver's ideas as pulp fiction did nothing to diminish their authoritativeness for readers, and this willingness to ignore fictional form in favor of factual essence is not unique. Other examples include claims that Edward Bulwer-Lytton's utopian tale, *The Coming Race*, is the true story of an underground world, and that Ayn Rand's gargantuan novel, *Atlas Shrugged*, is really the secret codebook of the Illuminati conspiracy. UFO enthusiasts have been particularly active proponents of the view that popular films such as *E.T.* are deliberately constructed messages to prepare the public for alien contact, a claim made by John Lear in the statement discussed earlier.[35]

Such fact-fiction reversals simultaneously diminish and expand the raw materials available to construct belief systems. They encourage one to dismiss what appear to be authoritative statements and interpretations, since those bear the stigma that attaches to all ideas associated with existing centers of power. At the same time, deviant views automatically become credible by virtue of their rejection. Contemporary millenarians draw disproportionately from ideas dismissed by mainstream institutions as illegitimate or simply false. This is notably true of the material I have been considering here, which leans heavily on such disreputable sources as hollow earth theories. Such material is drawn from what Colin Campbell refers to as the "cultic milieu" and what I have elsewhere called the "domain of stigmatized knowledge claims."[36] Both refer to beliefs that mainstream institutions – those that customarily validate truth claims – ignore or reject.

To an increasing extent, contemporary millenarians build their systems out of such material. In so doing, they tend to be indiscriminate borrowers, drawn to ideas as much by their rejected status as by their compatibility with other ideological elements. As a result, an increasing number of millenarian and apocalyptic belief systems are patchworks sewn together from disparate and seemingly incompatible materials. In the case I have been describing, the ingredients range from deviant science and theosophy to fringe Bible commentary and fantasy literature.

Those who have constructed this pastiche function less as prophets or ideologues than as bricoleurs, drawing on whatever components attract them and come to hand. This is what I mean by the "improvisational millenarian style."[37] Unlike earlier millennialists (and some present ones) who work within single coherent religious or ideological traditions, many contemporary millenarian entrepreneurs feel free to build systems out of bits and pieces that would not normally be joined together. It is, therefore, perhaps not accidental that so much of the material I have been concerned with appears first on the Internet, where dissimilar motifs can readily cohabit.

The current politicization of themes from science fiction, occultism, and other improbable sources is therefore at once surprising and entirely predictable – surprising in that none of this material is intrinsically political, but predictable in a situation in which millenarian bricoleurs combine elements with total freedom. Unconstrained by the discipline imposed by any single religious or secular belief system, they can range as widely as they like in search of material. Such indiscriminate borrowing has been facilitated by changes in the technologies of communication and reproduction.

Tales that first appeared as merely harmless and innocent confections about imaginary worlds have, therefore, become part of the New World Order apparatus of hidden, malevolent power that supposedly threatens human destiny; and underground fantasy worlds have become the locales for an imminent Armageddon.

NOTES

1. John Lear, "Statement Released by: John Lear December 29, 1987," in William F. Hamilton III, *Alien Magic* (Glendale, Calif.: Uforces, 1989), 1–7. The statement has been posted and reprinted many times, most recently in "Branton" (pseud.), *The Dulce Wars: Underground Alien Bases and the Battle For Planet Earth* (New Brunswick, N.J.: Inner Light/Global Communications, 2000), 22–35.

2. Jason Bishop, "The Dulce Base," in Hamilton, *Alien Magic*, 1 (the pagination in Hamilton is consecutive only within each section).

3. David Icke, *The Biggest Secret* (Scottsdale, Ariz.: Bridge of Light Publications USA, 1999), 125.

4. E.g., http://www.reptoids.com.

5. Icke, *The Biggest Secret*. More recently, two book-length manuscripts that initially appeared on web sites have now been published. Both are authored by an individual known only as "Branton": "Branton," *The Dulce Wars*; and "Branton," *The Omega Files: Secret Nazi UFO Bases Revealed!* (New Brunswick, N.J.: Global Communications, 2000).

6. The most complete history of hollow earth speculation, albeit without the conventional scholarly apparatus, appears in Walter Kafton-Minkel, *Subterranean Worlds: 100,000 Years of Dragons, Dwarfs, the Dead, Lost Races, and UFOs from inside the Earth* (Port Townsend, Wash.: Loompanics, 1989).

7. H. P. Blavatsky, *Isis Unveiled* (Theosophical University Press Online Edition, 1999), 1:595; http://www.theosociety.org/pasadena/isis/iu15.htm.

8. J. Gordon Melton, *The Encyclopedia of American Religions* (Tarrytown, N.Y.: Triumph, 1991), 2:200–201.

9. *Rocky Mountain News* (Denver), 30 August 1946, 22. *Denver Post*, 15 February 1953, 1.

10. Donna Kossy, *Kooks* (Portland, Oreg.: Feral House, 1994), 124–27.

11. M. Doreal, "Mysteries of the Gobi" (Sedalia, Colo.: Brotherhood of the White Temple, Inc., n.d.), 6, 10.

12. M. Doreal, "Flying Saucers: An Occult Viewpoint" (Sedalia, Colo.: Brotherhood of the White Temple, Inc., 1992), 29, 47–50.

13. "Thoth the Atlantean," *The Emerald Tablets*, M. Doreal, "translator," tablet 8. I have not been able to locate the original printed version. It appears online: http://crystalinks.com/emerald.html.

14. Kafton-Minkel, *Subterranean Worlds*, 154.

15. Robert E. Howard, *Kull* (New York: Baen, 1995), 33–34, 37.

16. L. Sprague de Camp, *Lovecraft: A Biography* (Garden City, N.Y.: Doubleday, 1975), 397.

17. "The Observatory, by the Editor," *Amazing Stories* 21 (June 1947): 9.

18. Raymond Palmer, "The Shaver Mystery," in Timothy Green Beckley, *The Shaver Mystery and the Inner Earth* (Clarksburg, W.Va.: Saucerian Publications, 1967), 115–18.

19. "The Shaver Mystery," *Amazing Stories* 20 (August 1946): 160–61. Letter from "Dr. M. Doreal," *Amazing Stories* 20 (September 1946): 177–78.

20. "Discussions," *Amazing Stories* 21 (October 1947): 172. Letter from "W. C. Hefferlin," *Amazing Stories* 22 (January 1948): 162.

21. The most complete scholarly treatment of the place polar regions occupy in esoteric literature is Joscelyn Godwin, *Arktos: The Polar Myth in Science, Symbolism, and Nazi Survival* (Kempton, Ill.: Adventures Unlimited Press, 1996), 137 and passim.

22. "Michael X" (pseud. Michael Barton), *Rainbow City and the Inner Earth People* (reprint, Clarksburg, W.Va.: Saucerian Books, 1969).

23. Godwin, *Arktos*, 86–87. Nicholas Goodrick-Clarke, *The Occult Roots of Nazism: Secret Aryan Cults and Their Influence on Nazi Ideology, The Ariosophists of Austria and Germany, 1890–1935* (reprint, New York: New York University Press, 1992), 218. "Agharti" is merely one of many alternative spellings ("Agarti," "Agharta," etc.).

24. Ferdinand Ossendowski, *Beasts, Men, and Gods* (New York: E. P. Dutton, 1922).

25. Ibid., 312, 314.

26. Raymond Palmer, "The King of the World?" *Amazing Stories* 20 (May 1946): inside back cover.

27. Heinrich Hauser, "Agharti," *Amazing Stories* 20 (June 1946): 8–9.

28. Robert Ernst Dickhoff, *Agharta* (reprint, New York: Fieldcrest, 1965).

29. Kafton-Minkel, *Subterranean Worlds*, 184.

30. Dickhoff, *Agharta*, 32.

31. Ibid., 76.

32. Doreal, "Flying Saucers: An Occult Viewpoint," 47. Dickhoff, *Agharta*, 69, 79.

33. Michael Barkun, *Religion and the Racist Right: The Origins of the Christian Identity Movement*, rev. ed. (Chapel Hill, N.C.: The University of North Carolina Press, 1997), 160–61, 178.

34. Bradley Whitsel, "Escape to the Mountains: A Case Study of the Church Universal and Triumphant" (Ph.D. diss., Syracuse University, 1998).

35. Lear, "Statement Released by: John Lear December 29, 1987," 4.

36. Colin Campbell, "The Cult, the Cultic Milieu and Secularization," in *A Sociological Yearbook of Religion in Britain* (London: SCM Press, 1972), 5:119–36. Michael Barkun, "Conspiracy Theories as Stigmatized Knowledge: The Basis for a

New Age Racism?" in Jeffrey Kaplan and Tore Bjorgo, eds., *Nation and Race: The Developing Euro-American Racist Subculture* (Boston: Northeastern University Press, 1998), 58–72.

37. Michael Barkun, "Politics and Apocalypticism," in Stephen J. Stein, ed., *The Encyclopedia of Apocalypticism*, volume 3, *Apocalypticism in the Modern Period and the Contemporary Age* (New York: Continuum, 1998), 442–60.

DANCE OF THE EPHEMERAL: AUSTRALIAN ABORIGINAL RELIGION OF PLACE

DEBORAH BIRD ROSE

INTRODUCTION

The genius of Aboriginal Australians finds its greatest expression in a theory and practice of place. This is so in the art, which is all about place, origins, and connections. This is so in social organization, and underwrites contemporary claims to land and the proof of what is called in the courts "traditional ownership." The genius of place is at the heart of religion, defined as engagements with the origins and deep patterns and processes of the created world. At the heart of concepts of place is a system of embodied connectivities. This religion of place concerns consubstantialities, proximities, communication, and action.

This paper aims toward considering some of the implications for the sacred when it is immanent in and emerges from emplaced patterns of connection in this world. To achieve this aim I first consider place through specific Dreaming tracks and sites. From this analysis I turn to a discussion of life, death, and consubstantiality. From there I direct my attention to concepts of time. I will suggest that research which shifts the focus of place from the abstract to the particular also destabilizes conventional Western concepts of time. Drawing on the analysis of place, I imagine time in an actualized mode. This analysis enables me to return to issues of place with new questions, from which I develop my analysis of the sacred as the dance of the ephemeral. Much of my analysis focuses on action; I seek to communicate issues concerning the work of the world. This is work of both daily and ceremonial life; it is work that keeps the world alive. Life, I will be implying, is not given, but rather is a flourishing dynamic that needs to be charged up, and that loves and seeks more life.

Aboriginal people's culture of connectivity makes a demand on Western scholarship: if place as relationship and connection is not to be analyzed reductively, what concepts and language do we have for engaging in dialogical analysis? I draw primarily on the work of Gregory Bateson. For a scholar such as myself, one of the great obstacles to understanding is the West's atomistic legacy, a legacy that has marginalized (but not eradicated) motion, process, recursivity, and connection. In the latter half of the twentieth century, converging scholarship in cybernetics, systems theory, theoretical physics, and ecology has started to reshape how we think about the world and to give us a language for engaging with a postatomistic cosmology.[1] In addition, there is the West's "other" tradition, a marginalized legacy on which I also draw. I am not, of course, suggesting that Australian Aboriginal culture is either post- or pre-Newtonian/Cartesian; I would actively resist the universalizing tendency implicit in forcing another culture into a position defined by Western history. My modest assertion is that a culture of connectivity cannot be adequately apprehended through a cosmology of atomism. Therefore, I turn to current Western language of connectivity in seeking to communicate some understanding of Aboriginal place and spirituality.

Much of the contemporary theorizing about place builds on a presupposition that place is a cultural artifact: human endeavors to make the world meaningful do so culturally, by investing space with meaning (for example).[2] In contrast, Aboriginal Australians do not take this kind of human-centered view of place. They hold place to be the product of the lives of many living things, including extraordinary beings and nonhuman beings. I use the term "eco-place" to speak to a locatedness that is not human-centered and that is attentive to the many living things who participate in the life of a given place.

Aboriginal Australians were for some sixty thousand years or so nomadic hunter-gatherers. Their elaboration of place was accomplished through mobility. This fact confounds Western expectations; the place to look for elaborations of place, one might have thought, was among people who remained in place. Aboriginal people engage with a particular nomadic problematic: that of being here and not-here at the same time, of being both localized and mobile. As Stephen Muecke puts it: always here, and always on the move.[3]

The specific cases I discuss in this paper are drawn from my long-term research with Aboriginal people in the Victoria River valley of the Northern Territory of Australia (fig. 1). The river originates in the arid zone and winds its way northward to the Joseph Bonaparte Gulf and the Timor Sea. The region is part of the great savanna zone of the monsoonal north. White settlers established broadacres cattle ranches (stations of thousands of square miles) just over one hundred years ago. Overrunning the

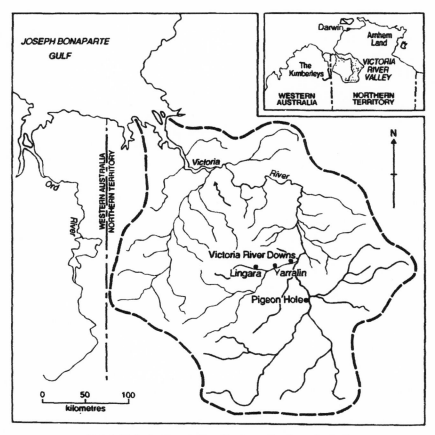

Fig. 1. Victoria River valley, Northern Territory, Australia

homes of the Indigenous peoples of the region, they first shot and hunted away the local peoples and later pressed them into service as an unfree and unpaid labor force.[4] In the mid-1960s Aboriginal people in this region went on strike against the appalling system of oppression which ruled their lives. Citizenship was granted in about 1969 and has enabled people to participate in national and international struggles for equity and cultural survival. Later, the Aboriginal Land Rights (Northern Territory) Act 1976 was passed, and while it has benefited some people far more than others, the material and political conditions of people's lives have been improved. All of my teachers worked in near slavery for white ranchers for greater or shorter periods of their lives; most went on strike, and all have achieved some measure of land rights.

TRACKS AND SITES

A fundamental proposition for Aboriginal concepts of place, as I have suggested, is that place is inseparable from motion. We should start with origins. Dreamings are the great creative beings who came out of the earth and traveled across the land and sea. The Australian continent is crisscrossed with the tracks of the Dreamings: walking, slithering, crawling, flying, chasing, hunting, weeping, dying, giving birth. They were performing rituals, distributing the plants, making the landforms and water, and making the relationships between one place and another, one species and another. They were leaving parts or essences of themselves; they would look back in sorrow; and then they would continue traveling, changing languages, changing songs, changing identity. They were changing shape from animal to human and back to animal again, and they were becoming ancestral to particular animals and particular humans (totemic groups). Through their creative actions they demarcated a world of difference and of relationships that crosscut difference: they are responsible for patterns and connections.

Dreamings are gendered – men and women, whether flying foxes, or possums, or human beings, traveled the earth creating a gendered landscape. The land does not privilege women to the exclusion of men, nor does it set women in opposition to men; rather, gendered land locates women and men separately as well as together. Secrecy preserves differ-

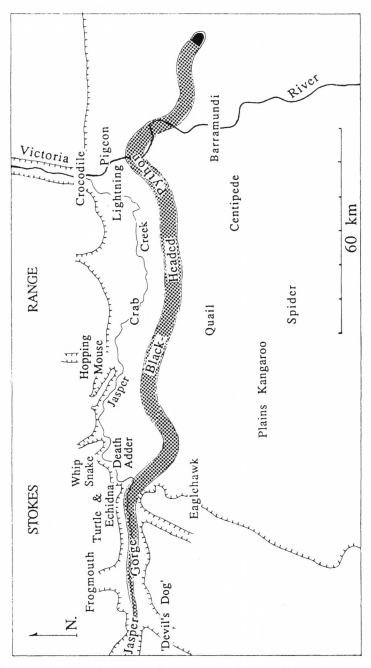

Fig. 2. The Black-headed Python in relation to some local Dreamings

ence, but much is not restricted by secrecy. I avoid secret matters for reasons of respect as well as ethics.

Dreamings established countries. A country is small enough to accommodate face-to-face groups of people and large enough to sustain their lives; it is politically autonomous in respect to other structurally equivalent countries, and at the same time it is interdependent with other countries. Each country is itself the focus and source of Indigenous law and life practice. As I have discussed in detail elsewhere, one's country is a "nourishing terrain," a place that gives and receives life.[5]

Dreamings traveled, and they stopped, and now they remain fixed in place, except under special circumstances, which I will discuss later. They stopped, they changed over into permanent sites or into other living things, and they stayed. Equally, however, they kept going. Dreamings are masters of the art of being here and not-here at the same time. They also are both then and now, both origins and contemporary presence. People interact with Dreamings in daily life as they do their hunting, fishing, gathering, visiting, and resting.[6] And people also interact with them in ceremonial contexts, which I will discuss briefly.

A country is rich in sentience. The Dreamings are there, of course, and so too are the dead people who belonged to the country in life. As I will discuss shortly, Dreamings left future generations of people in the country, and their yet-to-be-born sentience is also there. Animals are deemed to be sentient beings, as are some trees, rocks, and other sites; and then there are all the extraordinary beings. People call out to country, and if they did not do so it would be a sign that they were sneaking around. The country, defined as a nexus of sentience and communication, would know and respond, just as it is held to know and respond when the proper people address it in the proper way.

In considering eco-place, we have to be attentive to scale. Each country contains a plurality of sites, and many of the sites are connected by tracks; the ceremonies and ecologies that are part of the tracks work across bounded countries. The system of eco-places thus works with the embedded scales of sites within countries and small countries within larger units. More importantly, the system of eco-places elaborates the intersecting and crosscutting patterns of connection between eco-places.

Figure 2 shows a major Dreaming track in relation to numerous localized Dreamings that are fixed within small areas. The major Dreaming intersects smaller areas, interacting with localized Dreamings. Place and motion thus work together as one of the great patterns of the world: the here and not-here of life.

Figure 3 shows a selection of some of the major Dreamings in the Victoria River valley. The Dreamings are shown in relation to language boundaries: the stippled lines demarcate "tribal" (language group) boundaries. One of the key points to be drawn from this diagram is that it is not the case that everything is directly connected to everything else. Total interconnection would be physically impossible at scales larger than the extremely local and, equally importantly, would tend to undermine the system of difference on which connectivities are based. The other side of this factor is that nothing is unconnected, or, to put it another way, everything is connected to something that is connected to something, and so on across the continent.

The Black-headed Python is a woman Dreaming. She traveled from the sea in Western Australia to the sea off the coast of Queensland, a distance of hundreds of miles. Dreamings were shape-shifters. The Black-headed Python walked sometimes in the shape of a snake and sometimes in the shape of a woman. In snake form she was huge, and her slithery track carved out the river bed and the gorges that are pushed up on either side. The twists and turns of river and cliffs are the literal track of her passage in snake form. In her human form she carried a coolamon that was full of her foods, the seeds of which she distributed as she went along. Resource sites and resource-defined regions in this area owe their existence and their organization to the Python.

She also carried her children, and these, too, she kept leaving behind. Some of these children are the ancestors of the Aboriginal people who now own specific portions of the Black-headed Python track. The Python was generative in the sense of distributing plants into their proper habitats and into their associative biotic communities. She created an order marked by boundaries, concentrations, and associations. She was generative also in another sense: where she spoke a particular language, that language became the language for that country, and her songs are the songs of a major restricted ceremony. She was a woman, and so she gave birth – to the people of the country and, as I understand it, to the languages and the Law of the country. Many of the places where she stopped during her travels are "sacred sites" (the term is the accepted official and

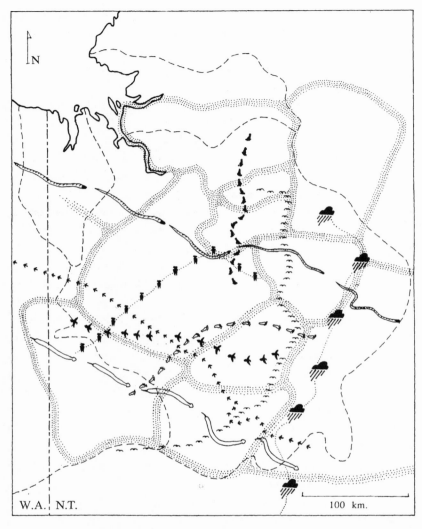

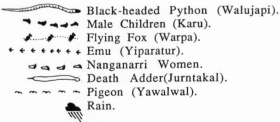

Black-headed Python (Walujapi).
Male Children (Karu).
Flying Fox (Warpa).
Emu (Yiparatur).
Nanganarri Women.
Death Adder(Jurntakal).
Pigeon (Yawalwal).
Rain.

Fig. 3. A selection of major Dreamings in the Victoria River valley

colloquial designation). Sites where she engaged in her generative action are sources of life. Life continues to emerge from these sites still today. In addition, she herself is still there. When we visited one of the main sites, the traditional owners called out to her, telling her who we were and why we were there.[7]

The Black-headed Python track demarcates both motion (her travels) and place (her sites, her boundaries). Her interactions with localized Dreamings put motion in connection with locatedness, and value both. Her generative actions create a world of form: the twisting river and steep-sided gorges are literal tracks, and other sites show physical evidence of her actions. She also creates a world of difference: here one language, there another; here one kind of tree, there another. She also created associations: here this community of plants that grow together in this habitat, there another plant community. Every one of these generative acts is termed "Law" in Aboriginal English. Law thus includes the origin of the shape of the country, the language for the country, and the plants and other living things for the country. But, as some of my Aboriginal teachers told me again and again to be sure that I would get it, "really Law" or "really culture" is the connections. Certain people belong to this country; they eat these foods, speak (or own) this language, know these places, perform these rituals, take care of these places, live under the Law of these connectivities, and work to hold them all together.

RETURNS

I turn now to a site on the track of the Nanganarri women (fig. 3). I documented many of the sites along a segment of this track belonging to my friend and teacher Ivy Kulngarri. Her country is defined as Bilinara language, and she is the boss for women's sites in the country and is one of the main bosses for sites along her section of the Nanganarri track, whether they be restricted or open. We documented sites for registration under the Aboriginal Areas Protection Act of the Northern Territory (formerly the Sacred Sites Act), and we also documented these and other sites as part of the evidence that was presented in the Bilinara land claim.[8]

This group of powerful Dreaming women, the Nanganarri, traveled, provided food, sang, did ceremony, and gave birth. Like the Python, they

carried plants, made places, brought language, and left the future generations of people in the country (fig. 4). Part of their ceremony is for making little boys into young men (first stage of male initiation).

There is one particular billabong where the Nanganarri women
stopped to bathe and rest. Ivy took me there, and when we approached
this place we saw the remains of an old campfire. Lying on the ground
among the charred sticks were the rusting remains of some burned tin
cans. I felt shocked: rubbish, litter, and junk right here at the place where
the Nanganarri women walked and where they are, still, today. Ivy looked
at the tin cans and she burst into a happy smile. She pointed to the remains of the fire and she explained:

> That fire, we had a dinner camp, oh, long time now, we came
> walkabout, and we got fish, and we had a dinner camp. You remem-
> ber Roy, my son Roy? Roy was here that day. We had a dinner camp
> here, we got fish, and we had damper and tea, and fish. Only Roy,
> Roy had a tin of beans. That tin there now, Roy had that one, baked
> beans. We had dinner camp right here, and Roy had that baked
> beans.

Fig. 4. Ivy Kulngarri, her daughters, and some granddaughters holding a stone that
contains future generations of their people. (Photo: Deborah Rose)

After, when we went back, they grabbed Roy, and took him away for young men's business. You remember that ring place [ceremony], Debbie? You were here then.[9]

This is a Dreaming place, and it is Ivy's home. She lives in her country, raises her family here, does her Law business here. The remains of the fire tell an intimate story about Ivy and her son Roy and their fishing trip. It is a story of kinship and nurturance; Ivy nurtured her children, and their country nurtured them all. It is also a story of care: they were here because they have responsibilities here. This is where they belong. The story already contains the histories of these people: Roy's origin in the site where the Nanganarri women left the people for this country, Ivy's work to bear and nurture him, Ivy's own origin in that Dreaming site, and her mother's work to bring her into the world and teach her how to live. Ivy was doing the work of the world: visiting country, feeding her family, teaching them, talking to country, interacting with it. When they went there that day, she would have called out to the country and to the dead people, saying: "Here we are, I've brought the kids, we're hungry." She is a senior person and has been here many times; the country would know them and would feed them. We know that they were cared for: the remains of the fire tell us so.

Ivy made the fire here quite a few years ago. She knew, but Roy did not, that this was Roy's last day as a child, so this is also a story about gender and law. The story reaches out through space to neighboring communities and neighboring countries. Many people came to work to make Roy into a young man. Perhaps Ivy had taken him walkabout to get him away from the community; perhaps she wanted a last day with her little boy. When they returned to camp, Roy was grabbed.

This story reached out and grabbed me as well. A few days after they took Roy, they brought him up to Victoria River Downs, and the mob I was living with then went over for the business. We did the farewell ceremony that separated Roy from his mother as a little boy. Ivy and all her sisters, daughters, cousins, and other women relations danced him goodbye. After the farewell, we had to work, and work, and work. Along with a lot of women, I danced all night to effect Roy's transformation from little boy to young man. The men sang, and we danced. They sang the songs of the Nanganarri travels, calling the places, and we danced the Dreamings through the country. In dance, the Dreamings travel again. Every ceremony is performative – it brings the Dreamings up out of the ground and carries them through the country. Ceremony keeps Dreamings in motion, it keeps the country charged up, and it transforms people. When Roy was returned to his relations weeks later, he was not a little boy any more.

I have suggested that Aboriginal people live with an enduring paradox: how to be here and not-here at the same time. The places in Ivy's country, and indeed her country itself, are constituted through both presence and memory. The traces that remain when the person who made them is gone are both sign and promise: living things return, and leave again. Country holds time and stories together; to live morally one must return, and return again. Thus, every return is a moral action, a promise fulfilled. Evidence of presence lies in the tracks and traces; knowledge constitutes proof. Ivy's knowledge of the tin cans was proof that she had been before, and thus had returned.

The signs of that day tell us that Ivy does not erase herself. Rather, she announces herself. Her footprints, her fires, her songs and stories, her visits, and her calling to the country are all communicative acts. They work within the broader communicative system of country, and they intend to be noticed. When we documented sites, we worked with Ivy's responsibilities for care and with a decolonizing agenda that would restructure some elements of power under colonialism; when Ivy went for her own sake she went in response to country. She knew what was happening in her country, and she knew where to go. The country communicated to her, and she took notice and responded. Her return was such a response.

DEATH, LIFE, AND CONSUBSTANTIALITY

I have offered examples of the great Dreaming women both because as a woman I know more about them and because I have wanted to convey the concept that women's generative power is a force for bringing the world into life. Just as birth is about place and metamorphosis, so too is death. At death the person is believed to become partitioned: the bones go back to the person's country, and some form of the person also returns to and travels in the person's country. When Ivy called out to her ancestors, saying that she wanted food for the kids, she was speaking to living presences in the country. Bones and ancestral presences contribute to the country's capacity to nourish the living generations. Death, when managed properly, is another form of return, and in the return death becomes another form of nurturance, which is to say that it fosters life.

These generalized propositions concerning death and birth elucidate structure, but not embodiment. Dreamings instituted relationships of consubstantiality. Anthropologists call these relationships (often described as categories) "totems." In the Victoria River valley, there is a multiplicity of types of totems; they consist in relationships of shared flesh, or shared body, between people and specific other species, and between people and their country. These relationships, too, intersect, overlap, and crosscut. People who are "countrymen" (the term refers to women and men) share their being with their country, and when the country suffers, so do people. Likewise, when people die, their country suffers. People identify marks, such as dead trees, scarred trees, or scarred hills, for example, as having come into being because of the death of a person who was associated with that country. Similarly with Dreamings: when Dreaming sites are damaged, people die; when people die, their Dreamings are at risk. Registering sites for protection under Anglo-Australian law was for Ivy a form of action in which care of others was also care of self.

The person who exists in others, and in whom others exist, is vulnerable to what happens outside his or her own skin, but that same person finds power in the relationships that are situated beyond the skin. Totemic and country relationships distribute subjectivity across species and countries such that one's individual interests are folded within, and realized most fully in the nurturance of, the interests of those with whom one shares one's being. The work of the world is based on and accomplished through interdependence.

TIME

Before venturing into time I will summarize the key points concerning place:
- Dreamings are about life in this world; Dreaming creation is localized, detailed, intimate, and connective; it is also in motion.
- There is no other world; this is immanence, not transcendence.
- Life comes into the world in its particularity. Whether looked at as

country or person, life is patterned into crosscutting, intersecting, and replicating shapes, connections, and relationships.

• The world is in motion, and the return is a responsive act of morality. The related point is this:

• Life involves change; change works through both place and time.

There are three main scholarly approaches to questions of Aboriginal time concepts. The first is the classic religious studies approach, which contrasts mythic time with historical time, sets Aborigines in a domain of mythic time, and defines it as eternal and unchanging. The concept depends on a distinction between sacred and profane, and is closely associated with Mircea Eliade's concept of Great Time,[10] although it should be noted that Eliade takes a more processual approach to the sacred in his study of Australian Aborigines.[11] The stately grandeur of mythic time requires humanity's submission and repetition, or, in Marcel Gauchet's terms, a passivity and dependence.[12] Loren Eiseley put this view eloquently in his essay on effacing time:

> [Primitive man] in his human time, subsists also in a kind of surviving dreamtime which is eternal and unchanging. Both men and animals come and go through the generations a little like actors slipping behind the curtain. . . . Sacred time is of another and higher dimension than secular time. It is, in reality, timeless; past and future are contained within it. All of primitive man's meaningful relationship to his world is . . . a mythical ordering of life which has not deviated and will not in future deviate from the traditions of eternity.[13]

A second approach takes stasis even further and denies that Aboriginal people have any time concepts.[14] Tony Swain contends that Aborigines "did not understand their being in terms of time" at all. His analysis seeks to erase time as a meaningful category in Aboriginal culture and to put total privilege on place and space. He hypothesizes a transcontinental ontology of place, and he further hypothesizes that this intellectual focus on place led Aborigines to deny both time and their own bodies.[15] The lack of time led them to avoid questions of cosmogony and first origins.[16] Swain was prepared to concede that Aboriginal people had a sense of rhythm and, indeed, recognized patterned rhythmic events.[17] He was not, however, prepared to consider that patterned action and rhythmic events might indicate forms of time.

A third approach assumes that Aboriginal time concepts can be equated at some level with Western time (that is, they are not wholly different), but that time is subordinated to space.[18] In this view, time-space coordinates exist, but spatial referents take precedence over temporal ones.

Each approach poses problems. Great Time is treated as if it were a form of eternity; it can be read as a denial of time. In its majesty it leaves little scope for the actual unfolding of life into place, nor does it offer a nuanced concept of contingency. There have been serious efforts to rescue the concept of mythic time from stasis,[19] but to the best of my knowledge, concepts of eternity, immutability, or archetypal action do not adequately engage with the perilous fragility and contingency of the created world. Similarly, the idea that Aborigines do not have a time concept rests on far too narrow a concept of time. Swain defines time in geometric terms: he asserts that numbered intervals are necessary not only to linear time, but to any notion of time,[20] and he makes a point of the fact that most Aboriginal numbering systems are limited. It is unarguable that if time is denied, bodies and cosmogonies become problematic, but it is not unarguable that only one kind of time exists in the world, or even in the Western world. As is well known, many contemporary studies of time look to heterogeneity: ecological time, genealogical time, evolutionary time, seasonal time, and others.[21] To restrict time concepts to mathematics is self-limiting; it does not rest well with the human experience of time (Henri Bergson's "real duration"), or with theoretical physics and the idea that matter consists of knots or sticky bits in time-space. Neither intuitively, theoretically, methodologically, nor ethnographically is there support for the denial of a time concept.

The third approach, that time is subordinate to space resonates with my experience and with that of many scholars who have lived and worked with Aboriginal people. In an earlier work I developed a broad formulation in respect of historical time. I suggested that historical/genealogical time is managed in the service of place and morality rather than in the service of chronology.[22] I would now suggest that the problem is more interesting than I then allowed for. This is the problem as I now see it:

1. Concepts of eco-place exist outside of the abstract concept of space

and are oriented toward the particular, the local, the connected, and the consubstantial.

2. Is time particularized in a comparable way? If the world can be talked about abstractly as comprised of time and space (or time-space), and if in Aboriginal people's specifics of the real world eco-place constitutes the spatial dimension, does some kind of real time constitute the temporal dimension?

I will suggest that motion instantiates the particularized quality of time. I am inspired here by Bergson's insights into the heterogeneity of time, into time as motion, and his conception of immanence as a ceaseless becoming.[23] Here, too, I will particularize. What I am calling the work of the world is work that ensures that motion is not just random movement, but rather consists of departures and returns. I will suggest that life is organized into patterns of connectivity that resolve themselves around interconnected eco-places, and that the meshing of personal, seasonal, ecological, generational, and ceremonial rhythms constitutes the heart of life, including the religious life, of the real world. Thus, I want to consider two interrelated time concepts: duration, defined by motion through real country, and the rhythms of the here and the not-here, the departure and return.

Fiona Magowan's exquisite essay "Crying to Remember" links song with eco-place in a mutual dance of memory: song evokes place, place evokes song, together they constitute relationships through time. Performance in place unfolds in time and draws other times – recent past and creation events – into a shared performative present.[24] Her work connects the scholarship of memory with concepts of local place.[25] Similarly, I suggest, the charred sticks and tin cans at the billabong hold a story that calls time into place. Ivy and Roy, and that fishing trip, are inscribed in this place for as long as the traces remain. Ivy occupies country not just by walking through it but by inscribing in it the passage of her life. The country holds her presence in the face of her absence (although not forever).

Eco-place is a fundamental time-space knot, a site of connectivities situated in real place and real time. Scholars such as Paul Shepard and Loren Eiseley use the technical concept of time binding to refer to a temporal situatedness in which past and present are both distinguished and co-present.[26] Alfred Schutz carries this work to a greater depth by showing how, through the experience of music, several dimensions of time can be not only copresent but shared. He thus offers an intersubjectivity that binds time to shared experience through the "possibility of living together simultaneously in specific dimensions of time."[27] In eco-place, both actual presence and signs of former presence are required; the recursions bind living things into time and place, as they bind time and place into the lives of living things, and enable intersubjectivities that are entirely situated.

In the world of change, where everything is in the process of becoming different to what it was, one of the great philosophical questions is: what is the quality of change? The philosopher Lev Shestov addresses this issue in a remarkable essay entitled "Children and Stepchildren of Time: Spinoza in History."[28] He contends that mainstream Western philosophy for more than two thousand years has identified as one of its two main projects to love that which is immutable and eternal. A love for the immutable is, in Western philosophy, a lack of love for, or indeed a denigration of, the ephemeral world that lives through change. Thus, time and change are the poor relations of Western philosophy, and so, too, is the world. As Shestov puts it: ". . . those who have meditated on this question have established . . . so strict a bond between the idea of death and the idea of change that the two ideas at present are only one. That which changes now appears as insignificant, as miserable, as that which is condemned to die."[29] Shestov's argument is against this focus on death and toward a focus on birth as the critical moment of our lives. He equates eternity with death and values birth as the entry of living things into time and motion.[30]

Aboriginal people also consider change. They treasure change in both time and place for the minimal reason that both are expressions of life, and they charge up the passion and moral presence of the changing through their emphasis on the return. To change is to move; to bring change into nurturance is to return. Birth is a key moment in place because it defines the source, and thus the site of return – to be born from a place is to be located so that one knows to where one shall return. The point of departure is the point of return. Within the scale of a human or nonhuman life, departures and returns are beats in the rhythm of country. The interplay between the here and the not-here, the beat and the interval, is movement that unfolds into real time.

Not only humans, but other living things do this too – they depart and return in a system of patterned connections. For example, the sun and rain in these monsoonal tropics take it in turn to dominate the sky, land, and waters. If there were only sun, everything would die of thirst, and if there were only water everything would drown. Within this big sequence there are simultaneities. When the cicadas call out, the turtles are getting fat, and when a particular riverine tree flowers, the barramundi are biting.[31]

Living things communicate by their sounds, their smells, their actions, the piercing song of cicadas, a flower floating in the water. They also communicate by their nonpresence. Events that occur to the same rhythm require intervals of nonoccurrence. There are times when things do not happen, and it is the not-happening that makes it possible for the happening to have meaning. The cicadas are only remarkable because for a long time they have been quiet. The beat of simultaneity is made possible by intervals of nonpresence or pause. People and other living things join the rhythms of eco-place through their own returns and departures, their beats and intervals. This is the daily "dance" of the ephemeral – living things are producing the patterns and rhythms of life in the world through their actions and interactions. This is to say that living things sustain the life of the world minute by minute as they live their patterned connections.

Life in the world of ephemeral, mobile, and changing beings exists within the ever-present possibility of slipping into disorder. Patterns, as I understand my Aboriginal teachers, are achieved, not given once and for all. Part of the work of the world is the work of connecting place and motion through the return. Recurrence is essential to what people talk about when they say that they work to keep the country alive.

Every place has a story; stories are located but not static. They pull people, other species, and other places into connection. Eco-place can thus be understood as an "attractor." The attraction is sensuous and is embodied in the ephemeral. Ephemeral beings respond, the responses are embodied action, the patterns are recursive, and time is bound into place, as life is bound into place, as place nurtures life.

This returns me to ceremony. One of Australia's greatest ethnomusicologists, Catherine Ellis, studied song performances in the context of the great ceremonies like those carried out by the Nanganarri women. Ellis analyzes the complex interlocking of a multiplicity of patterned elements: from the smallest element of the fixed duration of the short notes setting the song text, through the beating duration, the repeated rhythmic segments, rhythmic patterns, text presentations, to melody, small song, and song lines – each uses its own time-scale, and each relies on a series of intermittently emphasized patterns such that first one, then another, occupies the center of attention.[32]

Each element has its own pattern, and the genius of Aboriginal performers is to interlock all these multiple patterns. Ellis contends that Aboriginal people have the time equivalent of the gift we know as perfect pitch. Some Aboriginal performers are masters at organizing patterns in advance so that mathematically complex divisions fall correctly into the total pattern. This is done without reference to mathematics, and thus depends on some other faculty, which Ellis labels "perfect time."[33]

In Ellis's view, the correct interlocking of all of the patterns generates the power of song to draw the Dreamings out of the earth.[34] Ceremonies, I suggest, bind the time and motion of life back into place. And at the same time, they bring the power of the source out into the world. In ceremony, place is brought into the ritual ground through song, and place, ephemeral life, and enduring source are meshed into the time of the music and dancing so that motion flows in generative waves of becoming.

CONCLUSION: THE SACRED

The West's long history of equating the sacred with the eternal and immutable ill equips us to imagine another world in which life is valued for its qualities of birth, change, motion, death, temporality. I am proposing a very modest working definition that emerges from my engagement with eco-place. The sacred is that motion between the potential and the actual; it is the bringing forth of life into patterns and connections. To put it poetically, the sacred is the dance of the ephemeral. I do not intend to undermine existing concepts of static or enduring forms of the sacred. The "sacred sites" are sources, reservoirs of potential and templates of patterns. People's desire to protect these places is real and serious. I am suggesting, however, that sites are only part of the story. The other part is the work of the world, carried out by the ephemeral. This work brings potential into actual, and holds the actual in patterns that enable life to flourish. The work of the ephemeral thus charges up the potency of place and binds time into place through the returns that constitute a significant part of the moral order of the world.

Place, while wondrously dense, is also immensely vulnerable, because the ongoing life of the place happens through the actions of ephemeral living beings. What this means is that life doesn't just happen to happen. And it doesn't just happen to work itself into patterns, and it doesn't just keep returning like an automaton. Ephemeral beings are the crucial actors in all these processes: bringing life forth, sustaining patterns, returning and returning, in life and in death. Thus, the time-space matrix of the living world is a set of eco-places in which life is brought into time, and in which time and life are bound into place. The ephemeral dances itself returning through time into place. And returns sustain country as a nourishing terrain – as a place that gives and receives life.

I will conclude with a few points that start from the proposition that the sacred is a dance that requires a plenitude of living things in their specificity of place and motion to charge up patterns and connections by recursively binding life, time, and motion into place. From this starting point, one's responsibilities toward life are most properly understood as responsibilities toward emplaced connections. This analysis lifts issues of justice from the level of the individual to a much more focused and interactive level of place and connection. It follows from here that both human rights and animal and ecosystem rights must be thought of more expansively and more specifically.

A great Arnhem Land thinker, whose words have been published by Ian McIntosh in his book *The Whale and the Cross*, said that the real human rights are the rights to learn about your country and to take care of your country and the life there.[35] This definition is profoundly countermodern: the rights to return, to protect, to take care, and to sustain connection all work against the transience and fragmentation of modern and postmodern society.[36]

I mentioned earlier that Shestov identified two great projects of Western civilization, one of which was its love of the immutable and the eternal. The other is its abhorrence of mystery. With his usual acerbity he stated: ". . . all the enigmas of being are still not solved. I say this only because it seems to me that it is always forgotten."[37] The project of eradicating mystery through reason has been greatly enhanced with the development of science from the Enlightenment to today, so it is a delightful paradox that good science is returning mystery to the world in the forms of relativity, complexity, and uncertainty. From my Aboriginal teachers I gained the desire to charge up mystery and to reinvigorate our sense of participating in a living world of passion, connection, pattern, and change. The world with its desire for connection calls us in particular ways that really matter. How we answer determines our ability to participate in and to love the nourishing dance that goes on all around us.

NOTES

I am grateful to the Center for the Study of World Religions for the opportunity to develop and present the ideas contained in this paper. The final version was researched and written during my tenure in the Centre for Resource and Environmental Studies at the Australian National University.

1. Freya Mathews, *The Ecological Self* (London: Routledge, 1991).

2. See, for example, Yi-Fu Tuan, *Topophilia: A Study of Environmental Perception, Attitudes, and Values* (Englewood Cliffs, N.J.: Prentice-Hall, 1974).

3. Krim Benterrak, Stephen Muecke, and Paddy Roe, *Reading the Country* (Fremantle, Australia: Fremantle Arts Centre Press, 1984), 3.

4. See Hobbles Danaiyarri in Deborah Rose, "The Saga of Captain Cook: Remembrance and Morality," in Bain Attwood and Fiona Magowan, eds, *Telling Stories* (Sydney: Allan and Unwin, 2001).

5. Deborah Rose, *Nourishing Terrains: Australian Aboriginal Views of Landscape and Wilderness* (Canberra: Australian Heritage Commission, 1996); and Emmanuel Levinas, *The Levinas Reader*, ed. Sean Hand (Oxford: Basil Blackwell, 1989), 210.

6. Elizabeth A. Povinelli, *Labor's Lot: The Power, History, and Culture of Aboriginal Action* (Chicago: University of Chicago Press, 1993).

7. Deborah Rose, "Flesh and Blood, and Deep Colonising," in *Claiming Our Rites: Studies in Religion by Australian Women Scholars*, ed. Morny Joy and Penelope Magee (Adelaide: Australian Association for the Study of Religions, 1994).

8. D. Rose and D. Lewis, *The Bilinara (Coolibah-Wave Hill Stock Route) Land Claim* (Darwin: Northern Land Council, 1989); Aboriginal Land Commissioner, *Bilinara (Coolibah-Wave Hill Stock Routes) Land Claim* (Canberra: Australian Government Printing Service, 1990).

9. Paraphrased from rough notes.

10. Mircea Eliade, *Patterns in Comparative Religion* (London: Sheed and Ward, 1958).

11. Mircea Eliade, *Australian Religions: An Introduction* (Ithaca, N.Y.: Cornell University Press, 1973).

12. Marcel Gauchet, *The Disenchantment of the World: A Political History of Religion*, trans. Oscar Burge (Princeton: Princeton University Press, 1999 [1997; 1985]), 7, 24.

13. Loren Eiseley, "The Time Effacers," in Loren Eiseley, *The Invisible Pyramid* (New York: Charles Scribner's Sons, 1970), 112–13.

14. Tony Swain, *A Place for Strangers: Towards a History of Aboriginal Being* (Cambridge: Cambridge University Press, 1993).

15. Ibid., 14.

16. Ibid., 32.

17. Ibid., 19.

18. For example, see W. E. H. Stanner, "The Dreaming," in *White Man Got No Dreaming: Essays, 1938–1973* (Canberra: Australian National University Press, 1979 [1953]), 23–40.

19. For example, David Abram, *The Spell of the Sensuous: Perception and Language in a More-than-Human World* (New York: Vintage Books, 1996), 186–87.

20. Swain, *A Place for Strangers*, 18.

21. B. Adam, "Running Out of Time: Global Crisis and Human Engagement," in Michael Redclift and Ted Benton, eds., *Social Theory and the Global Environment* (London: Routledge, 1994); and Ariel Salleh, *Ecofeminism as Politics: Nature, Marx, and the Postmodern* (London: Zed Books, 1997).

22. Deborah Rose, *Dingo Makes Us Human: Life and Land in an Australian Aboriginal Culture* (Cambridge: Cambridge University Press, 2000), 206–7.

23. Tom Quirk, *Bergson and American Culture: The Worlds of Willa Cather and Wallace Stevens* (Chapel Hill: University of North Carolina Press, 1990), 47–50.

24. Fiona Magowan, "Crying to Remember," in Bain Attwood and Fiona Magowan, eds., *Telling Stories* (Sydney: Allan and Unwin, 2001).

25. See Steven Feld for a similar analysis located in Papua New Guinea: Steven Feld, "Waterfalls of Song: An Accoustemology of Place Resounding in Bosavi, Papua New Guinea," in Steven Feld and Keith H. Basso, eds., *Senses of Place* (Santa Fe, N.M.: School of American Research Press, 1996).

26. Paul Shepard, *The Others: How Animals Made Us Human* (Washington, D.C.: Island Press/Shearwater Books, 1996), 16; and Eiseley, "The Time Effacers."

27. Alfred Schutz, "Making Music Together: A Study in Social Relationship," *Social Research* 18, no. 1 (1951): 76–97, quote p. 79.

28. Lev Shestov, "Children and Stepchildren of Time: Spinoza in History," in Bernard Martin, ed., *A Shestov Anthology* (Athens, Ohio: Ohio University Press, 1970).

29. Lev Shestov, *Athens and Jerusalem*, trans. Bernard Martin (New York: Simon and Schuster, 1968), 406–7.

30. In Bernard Martin, ed., *Great Twentieth-Century Jewish Philosophers: Shestov, Rosenzweig, Buber* (New York: Macmillan, 1970), 37.

31. Discussed in greater detail in Rose, *Dingo Makes Us Human*.

32. Catherine Ellis, "Time Consciousness of Aboriginal Performers," in Jamie C. Kassler and Jill Stubington, eds., *Problems and Solutions: Occasional Essays in Musicology Presented to Alice M. Moyle* (Sydney: Hale and Ironmonger, 1984), 155.

33. Ibid., 84.

34. Catherine Ellis, *Aboriginal Music: Education for Living* (St Lucia: University of Queensland Press, 1985), 109.

35. Ian McIntosh, *The Whale and the Cross: Conversations with David Burru-marra M.B.E.* (Darwin: Northern Territory Historical Society, 1994), 78.

36. Freya Mathews, "Letting the World Grow Old: An Ethos of Countermoder-nity," *Worldviews: Environment, Culture, Religion* 3, no. 2 (1990): 119–38.

37. In Martin, *Great Twentieth-Century Jewish Philosophers*, 117.

NOTES ON CONTRIBUTORS

Michael Barkun (Ph.D., Northwestern University) is Professor of Political Science in the Maxwell School at Syracuse University. His most recent book is *A Culture of Conspiracy* (University of California Press, 2003). Among his other publications are *Religion and the Racist Right*, which received the Myers Center Award; *Disaster and the Millennium*; and *Law without Sanctions*; together with numerous articles and book chapters. He has served as a consultant to the FBI on religious movements and has received grants and fellowships from the Harry Frank Guggenheim Foundation, the Ford Foundation, and NEH. He served as editor of *Communal Societies* and presently sits on the boards of *Terrorism and Political Violence* and the Center for Millennial Studies at Boston University.

Mary Gerhart is Professor of Religious Studies at Hobart and William Smith Colleges. The author of *Genre Choices, Gender Questions* (1992), she is coauthor (with Allan Russell, a physicist) of *Metaphoric Process: The Creation of Scientific and Religious Understanding* (1984) and *New Maps for Old: Explorations in Science and Religion* (2001). She has served as editorial chair of *Religious Studies Review* and on the editorial boards of several other journals.

Ann Grodzins Gold is Professor of Religion and Anthropology at Syracuse University. Gold's research in North India has included studies of pilgrimage, world-renunciation, women's expressive traditions, environmental change, and the transmission of environmental knowledge. Her publications include four books: *Fruitful Journeys: The Ways of Rajasthani Pilgrims*; *A Carnival of Parting*; *Listen to the Heron's Words: Reimagining Gender and Kinship in North India* (coauthored with Gloria Raheja); and *In the Time of Trees and Sorrows: Nature, Power, and Memory in Rajasthan* (coauthored with Bhoju Ram Gujar).

Mary N. MacDonald is a historian of religions who teaches at Le Moyne College in Syracuse, New York. She studies the religions of Oceania with a focus on styles of Christianity that have developed in Papua New Guinea and an interest in the relationship of ecology and religion.

Jacob K. Olúpònà is a historian of religions and is Professor of African American and African Studies at the University of California at Davis. He has taught and conducted research for many years in Nigeria and the United States. Among the several books he has written or edited are *Religion, Kingship, and Rituals in a Nigerian Community* (Almqvist and Wiksell, 1991), *African Spirituality: Forms, Meanings, and Expressions* (Herder and Herder, 2001), and *Beyond Primitivism: Indigenous Religious Traditions and Modernity* (Routledge, forthcoming).

Deborah Bird Rose is Senior Research Fellow at the Centre for Resource and Environmental Studies at The Australian National University. She is the author of *Nourishing Terrains: Australian Aboriginal Views of Landscape and Wilderness* (1996), *Dingo Makes Us Human* (winner of the 1992–93 Stanner Prize), and *Hidden Histories* (winner of the 1991 Jessie Litchfield Award). Her most recent book is *Country of the Heart*. Writing in the fields of anthropology, history, environmental ethics, and religious studies, her work is focused on social and ecological justice. Her current work in progress is a book entitled "Dreaming Ecology."

Nili Wazana (Ph.D., Hebrew University of Jerusalem) is Lecturer in the Departments of Bible and of the History of the Jewish People at the Hebrew University of Jerusalem. She examines biblical history and ideas in the light of contemporary documents from surrounding civilizations. Her published articles deal with the conception of territories and borders in the ancient Near East, reactions to cultural contacts reflected in the Bible, and with spatial and diachronic transition of literary traditions and motifs. She is currently preparing a book entitled "Borders of the Promised Land: The Language of Geographical Ideology."